Launch Your Online Course Business in 90 Days or Less
(start from scratch with minimal investment)

All rights reserved. No part of this publication may be reproduced or transmitted in any form or by any means, electronic or mechanical, including photocopying, recording, scanning, or otherwise, or through any information browsing, storage, or retrieval system, without permission in writing from the publisher.

DISCLAIMER AND/OR LEGAL NOTICES
While the publisher and authors have used their best efforts in preparing this book, they make no representation or warranties with respect to the accuracy or completeness of the contents of this book. The advice and strategies contained herein may not be suitable for your situation. The information and/or documents contained in this book do not constitute legal or financial advice and should never be used without first consulting with a professional to determine what may be best for your individual needs.

The publisher and the author do not make any guarantee or other promise as to any results that may be obtained from using the content of this book. You should never make any investment decision without first consulting with your own financial advisor and conducting your own research and due diligence. Adherence to all applicable laws and regulations, the publisher and the author disclaim any and all liability in the event any information, commentary, analysis, opinions, advice and/or recommendations contained in this book prove to be inaccurate, incomplete or unreliable or result in any investment or other losses.

Content contained or made available through this book is not intended to and does not constitute legal advice or investment advice, and no attorney-client relationship is formed. The publisher and the author are providing this book and its contents on an "as is" basis. Your use of the information in this book is at your own risk.

A Note to the Reader

Chapter 1: From College Professor to Online Entrepreneur

Chapter 2: How to Know If You're Ready to Start

Chapter 3: Defining Your Profitable Niche

Chapter 4: Building Your Audience

Chapter 5: Discover Your Profitable Course Idea

Chapter 6: Create Your Online Course

Chapter 7: Getting Your Online Course Ready to Sell

Chapter 8: How to Find Your Perfect Students

Chapter 9: Growing Your Online Course Business

Chapter 10: Sell Your Online Course on Autopilot

Chapter 11: #1 Skill Needed for Success

A Note to the Reader

This book will teach you how to build your online course business. If you are a freelancer, coach, teacher, or an expert in your field, or you simply have knowledge that you want to share with the world, creating an online course or membership will transform your life.

Before you spend thousands of dollars creating a product that has not been tested and validated, with this book, you'll learn how to set up your future online course business for success. You can do this all within 90 days with minimal investment.

Online courses allow you to share what you know, help others, and give you the freedom to work from anywhere in the world (and with tiny humans in your house).

Here is a word of caution. This book is all about taking action. This step-by-step playbook is not based on theory or hype but is driven by the author's experience in helping thousands of other course creators build their online businesses.

Throughout the book, I have provided examples of other online course creators at various stages of their business. These interviews are from my ordinary course creator interview series that I conducted for The Course Creator's MBA Podcast. You can check out these stories and others by subscribing on Apple Podcast or your favorite podcast platform.

As I always say, an online course business is 90% marketing and only 10% product creation. Let us get yours up and running in the next 90 days.

Chapter 1: From College Professor to Online Entrepreneur

This chapter title really should say "High-School Dropout to Online Entrepreneur." Yes, you read that right. The last full grade I completed in high school was 9th grade. If we're being technical, 9th grade was considered junior high, so I never completed a full grade in high school. But this is how my journey started.

I was always bored in school. Completely and utterly bored. Even in college at Clemson University, if I could get away with it, I would come to the first class, get the syllabus, find out when the assignments were due and make sure to show up on test day. I hated sitting through boring lectures. This is just between you and me — please, don't tell my kids this; I don't want them to think it's ok to skip class!

I've always been a self-learner. It's easy for me to read a book, retain the information, and implement it. I love to read, take classes, and learn about new things. That's why I love marketing; the field is constantly changing and evolving. When I left high school, I couldn't sit through class. I was bored and felt like I could learn the information on my own. Looking back, I don't feel like I lived up to my potential. I decided to take the GED and started a community school near where I lived, later transferring to Clemson University.

At this point in my life, I didn't know what I wanted to do; I just knew that I wanted to be in business. One of my college boyfriends asked me where I saw myself in 10 years. Immediately I said CEO of my own company — he broke up with me shortly after.

I majored in accounting in college, not because I loved accounting or numbers, but simply because I asked my advisor at Clemson what a good major would be, and he said, "Major in accounting. If you learn accounting, you can move into any business field."

I hated accounting. Journal entries bored me to death, and I hated working with spreadsheets all day. I only lasted 1 ½ years in that role. I got a job at a start-up working in finance as an analyst. It was an interesting job, and I learned a lot about putting together financial forecasts.

BTW, by this point, I was pregnant with my first child at 25 years old. My husband and I had been married for about three years (I got married two weeks after I graduated from Clemson). We were already in our second home and had built a pretty good life for a young couple. We were still located in the Greenville, SC area, and things were going pretty well.

However, I was bored at work. Again. A position in marketing came up at the start-up; I interviewed and got the job. My whole world changed. I love marketing. I love the challenges it brings; how you have to test, tweak and test and tweak. There really are no silver bullets, and every product and business is different. This was a pivotal point in my career, but there was one thing that was missing.

Chris, my significant other, and I realized that we needed to live near a big city for our careers. I started searching and found a job with BellSouth (now part of AT&T) in their new Internet services division. I went down to Atlanta to interview for the marketing position and was offered the job during the interview that day. We packed up and moved to Atlanta in October of 1998.

Fast forward five years, during my tenure at BellSouth, I started as an Asst. Product Manager, moved to Product Manager, then Sr. Product Manager, and later was promoted to Director in Product Management. We had some fun times during this time. Internet services were in the growth stage, and marketing was fun and challenging at the same time. During these five years, I had my second child and completed my MBA.

I worked hard and played hard. In 2003, BellSouth started to plan the merge with AT&T. I was burned out and ready for a change. The first round of layoffs and packages came and went. Then the second round. I didn't receive a package. I was ready to do something different and raised my hand and asked for a package and was given one. This was another turning point in my career.

I took one year off after leaving BellSouth. I had two small children, wanted to get in shape and spend time with my kids whom I felt like I had neglected after years of working long hours. I took up tennis and was addicted!

I learned quickly that being a stay-at-home mom wasn't for me. I started researching possible opportunities and what I wanted to do next. I researched the possibility of starting a coaching business and even bought a domain name. It wasn't as easy as it is now to get started. Social media hadn't taken off, and DIY website builders weren't mainstreamed.

I found an online advertisement where a university was looking for online (virtual) business instructors. I love teaching and helping others, so I applied and was hired. This was when online learning at the university level was just taking off. I started teaching marketing online for the university and was later hired as a full-time faculty member. My career at the university was off to a good start. I did several jobs over the next 12 or so years, ranging from an adjunct faculty, full-time faculty, Program Director, Asst. Dean, Associate Vice Chancellor of Academic Affairs, just to name a few. Oh, and I had two more kids during this time.

What do you think happened? Yep, you're right. I got burned out but most importantly had this itch that I couldn't scratch. I had always wanted to start my own business. At this point, I didn't have a good idea of what I wanted to do, but here's what I did know.

I loved teaching online, I loved marketing, and I loved helping others. This is how my online course business got started. I stopped and started several different careers during my journey to get to where I am today. Now, let's create your story.

Chapter 2: How to Know If You're Ready to Start

Market Opportunity for Online Learning

The global e-learning market is projected to grow tremendously over the next few years, with an astounding projection of $375 billion by 2026. Today, roughly 90% of corporations use some form of e-learning compared to 4% in 1995. Due to the global pandemic, companies, educational institutions, and governments have had to re-evaluate how they conduct business. Even everyday people who want to learn a new skill or participate in personalized learning seek different alternatives to traditional, face-to-face learning. With necessary restrictions and social distancing, the need for alternative solutions to education, training, and day-to-day business processes has become a must. Because of this, learning online has exploded as the new trend in learning and development, opening a tremendous opportunity for online course creators.

The market opportunities are not just limited to educational institutions or corporations. People are looking for courses on travel, health and wellness, home and leisure, art and music, technology, gaming web design, social media marketing, and personal development, to name a few. Most users look for content that's relevant to the subject that they are seeking to learn. Remote learning is also important because users want to be able to learn anywhere, at any time.

As an online course business, you don't need to create your online courses following multiple learning content trends. However, it's a good idea to know what options are available and the current trends in the market. Let's look at a few.

Microlearning, also called bite-size training, chunk learning, learning nuggets, you get the idea. This consists of short chunks of content delivered in modules, usually no longer than 10 minutes. It is designed to provide short bits of information that target a specific topic over a limited time frame. This is an incredible option for people on the go who don't have much time. They can complete one learning objective at a time and not become overwhelmed. This type of learning is effective in skill-based learning or training strategies.

Virtual Classroom Training is an online system in which students and instructors meet online to communicate and collaborate. These types of classrooms are usually cloud-based, operating as part of a learning management system. Virtual learning requires that the technology is working properly and accessible to people in remote locations. It can be more flexible than a traditional classroom and provides live interactions, ready-to-use features, the ability to collect immediate feedback, conduct polling, and administer tests in real-time.

Virtual Reality is a computer-generated method that allows a person to interact within a three-dimensional environment using electronic devices. Trending technologies are simulated in real-life situational learning or an imaginary learning environment. People often associate this virtual reality with video games; however, it can be used in other applications.

Gamification and Game-Based Learning is a learning trend in which users can learn through playing games. This type of learning can provide rules, competitions, point scoring, badges, and is especially successful in keeping users engaged.

Learning Experience Platforms deliver a personalized learner experience, a platform where exchanging subject-matter expertise is easy and open. This type of learning is popular in organizations that want to help their employees grow professionally, either productively, or in a profitable way, or both.

Video-Based Learning is often a preferred method to communicate crucial messages, provide safety training, or raise the awareness of an organization. It is a popular form among learners. It can be a combination of short, multiple videos that offer small nuggets of information that can be both self-running and interactive.

Social and Collaborative Learning is the type of learning where students interact with the instructors and other students to expand their knowledge. Essentially it is group-based learning. This approach encourages students to actively engage with other learners to process and synthesize information. This is done using projects that might demand students to defend a position, collaborate through forums, chat sessions, and so on. It forces students to get out of their comfort zone and open up. It can be a very effective form of team-building.

Now that we've reviewed many of the current trends, it's time to get started. You may have been thinking about it for a while—a little voice in the back of your head telling you it's time to share your knowledge with the world. Perhaps you're a teacher or a freelancer who wants to share their expertise with a larger audience through an online course, or even sell an e-book online. Or maybe you have a special skill or gift that you know you can monetize and use to help people at the same time. But how do you know if you're ready to take on the challenge of starting a new business?

Five Ways to Know If You're Ready to Start

You are creative and driven with the ability to get things done

As a business owner, you are the boss, the CEO of your company. You are responsible for marketing promotions, content creation, customer communications, new product development, and more. You must be able to do all of this while executing the day-to-day needs of your business.

You are willing to take risks

"He who is not courageous enough to take risks will accomplish nothing in life" — Muhammad Ali.

You are ready and willing to take on the challenge of running your own online business. You might hear that voice in your head saying things like: What if my idea won't work? What if I'm a failure? Can I even do this? There will always be fear of the unknown. Let me let you in on a little secret—you are not alone. Everyone, at some point, experiences the voice of self-doubt whispering in their ears. In fact, in a poll of 1,000 Americans, the top fear is personal failure.

You are patient

What if I build this business, but no one comes? Unless you are starting your business with an established audience, which is typically not the case, it will take a while for you to get up and running. You have to be patient, consistently deliver on your marketing plan, show up, and follow through. If you do this, you will be far ahead of most of your competition.

You are flexible and able to follow a plan

There is a systematic step-by-step process for coming up with business ideas. This includes finding your special gift or why you want to start your new business. How will you differentiate yourself or your product in the marketplace? Have you defined your business model and product offerings? Can you describe your ideal customer?

An important step is validating your idea and analyzing your results. Once you have your business idea, you will need to put a plan in place to execute. Flexibility is key. Your business will evolve over time based on your customers' needs and wants as you get to know them better.

You are willing to reach out for support and guidance

You are not in this all alone. There are many ways entrepreneurs can get support and guidance as they go through their journey. One of the best ways is to find a private Facebook or LinkedIn group similar to what you are interested in doing. They will be there for you when you stumble, eager to answer your questions and provide guidance along the way.

What is the lifestyle I wish to create?

Perhaps you have young children, and you're looking for a lifestyle that gives you the flexibility to spend more time at home. You may be someone who travels often and would like to work from anywhere in the world. Maybe you don't enjoy the 9-to-5 grind and have always dreamed of owning your own business where you can create your own hours. Sounds like a dream, right? Not really. You can create the lifestyle you desire. All you have to do is make that your focus.

Chapter 3: Defining Your Profitable Niche

You may think that to start your online course business you first need to create your course. Not so fast!

An online course is a product; it's what you sell. It's not your online course business. In fact, an online course business is only 10% product creation and 90% marketing. There is so much more you need to do before you start creating your first online course. The first step is to determine who you want to serve and how you can help them.

This is the hardest thing for entrepreneurs to figure out when they're just getting started. I've started working with clients who, before working with me, spent years spinning their wheels and getting nowhere because they couldn't figure this out. If this is where you've been struggling, it's completely normal.

Determine Who You Want to Serve and How You Can Help Them

There is a simple exercise you can do to figure this out. But I want you to remember this. Even if you decide who you want to serve and how you will help them, it doesn't mean that you can't pivot at any point in the future. In fact, I'm willing to bet you will pivot in your online course business several times over the next few years. And I'm here to tell you that's ok!

Most online course creators have a burning desire to help others. They are teachers at heart. They have a skill set that can help solve a real problem in the marketplace. Whether it is teaching others how to become a goat farmer or how to code, you want to meet a need and help others at the same time.

Consider your motivation for starting your online course business. Many people have this misconception that an online course business is easy money. They've heard the term passive income thrown around. An online course business is anything but easy money. Yes, you can make money on autopilot and while you're on vacation, but you'll have to invest time, energy, and effort into your business.

An online course business is a marketing machine, and it takes time to grow an online business just like it takes time to grow a brick-and-mortar business. If your sole motivation for starting your online course business is easy money, just stop here.

Figuring out who you will help and how you will help them is an evolving process. Even if you're not 100% sure about what exactly you want to do, pick a niche and move forward. Clarity comes from action. Once you build your audience and talk with your potential clients and customers, it'll become clear how you can help them.

You may also be worried that what you want to teach is already being taught by other online course creators. Then, I would say GOOD! Competition validates demand. There are many different clothing brands in the market, tons of fast-food restaurants, many different email-service providers, and video-conferencing apps. You will bring your own personal touch to your business and online course. Let me walk you through this simple exercise on how you can select your niche.

Step 1: Uncover Your Business Ideas Based on Your Passions, Skills, and Achievements

In this step, think about aspects of your current work or personal life where you could help people. Anything goes here! Grab a piece of paper and list any skill set or achievement that you've developed in school, work, or personal life.

If you're stuck, think about what you have accomplished so far in life. What do you enjoy doing? What are you passionate about? What doesn't feel like work? What do people ask you to help them with?

If you're anything like me, this is probably a huge list—see my list below. As you can see, in the picture below, under achievements, I've listed things like my management experience, work experience, and what I've accomplished in my personal life. For my skills, I've included my marketing and leadership skills, time and productivity management skills.

To come up with this list, I reviewed my resume and thought about the various work and volunteer positions I've had over the years. You can also think about your hobbies and where you spend most of your free time doing what you love.

Here's the list that I came up with:

Next, I want you to categorize these into possible business ideas. For instance, from my list, I came up with four possible business ideas based on my skills, achievements, and what I love doing. I've highlighted the one I'm most interested in pursuing.

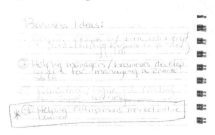

I'll let you in on a little secret. I have come close to starting all these businesses and may explore some of them in the future! But, at this point, I've decided to pick and focus my efforts on just one so I'm not spread too thin. Next, we'll get specific in narrowing down your niche.

Step 2: Identify Your Perfect Customer

In the next step, we'll identify your perfect customer, so you can speak directly to them. For your top business idea, what does your perfect customer look like? You will need to get very specific and identify one ideal customer profile for your course. **Big Hint:** It's not everyone, and it's not general. It's not just a stay-at-home mom or an entrepreneur.

You may be wondering, why is this important? Or you may be concerned that if you get too specific, your niche will be too narrow, and you'll lose out on business. When you're specific about who you want to help, it allows you to speak directly to that person.

Have you ever read something and thought, "Wow, that sounds exactly like me?" It's because they're speaking directly to one customer and not trying to be all things to all people.

Think about income, age, the websites they visit, their pain points, fears, frustrations, dreams, and desires. Consider the following:

- Age range
- Gender
- Where do they live?
- Marital status

- Education level
- What do they do for work?
- Where do they go for information?
- What influencers do they follow?
- What are their dreams and desires?
- What are their pain points and frustrations?
- What transformation do they want?
- Would or can they pay money to fix their issue?
- What keeps them up at night?
- What is their role in the purchase decision?
- What objections might they have?

Step 3: Conduct Research to Understand Your Perfect Customer

In this step, you'll conduct a competitive analysis. You're not doing this to copy your competitors, quite the opposite. You want to make sure you are differentiating yourself in the market.

What's a Competitive Analysis?

A competitive analysis is a review of your competitors. It's that simple. You are looking at how they are positioning themselves in the market and what they are doing right or doing wrong, so you don't make the same mistakes. It also allows you to identify gaps in the market, so you can help serve them.

How to Conduct a Competitive Analysis for Your Online Course

Make a List of Your Competitors

First, make a list of all your competitors. This list should include five or so competitors that you want to review. Put them in an Excel file or Google sheet so you can track what you discover. If you don't know who your competitors are for your online course, spend some time in Facebook or LinkedIn groups. Check out your Facebook or Instagram feed. Some of their ads are likely targeting you!

Next, you will review the following for each competitor and track your findings:

1. What lead magnet do they offer for their course?

2. What makes them unique? In other words, what is their positioning statement?

3. Sign up for their newsletter. What do they include in their emails? How often do they email their subscriber list?

4. Review their social media accounts. What social media accounts are they most active in? Are they posting regularly? How big is their following? How are they promoting their course on social media? Is the content original or curated from other sources?

5. Subscribe to their blog or podcast. Are they blogging regularly? How do they promote their content? Are users engaged with their content?

6. Review their pricing and what's included in their online course. What support do they offer students? How do they justify their pricing?

7. If applicable, read any customer reviews.

8. How do they promote their online course? Through emails, social media, ads?

9. Review their advertising. Save any Facebook or Instagram ads. What's included in their ad copy?

10. Are they using affiliates to sell their online course?

Conduct Your SWOT Analysis

SWOT stands for strengths, weaknesses, opportunities, and threats. Here, you will consider:

- What is your competition doing well? What are their strengths?

- Where do they have room for improvement? Did you identify any weakness in their business or with their online course?

- Based on your review, what opportunities can you take advantage of?

- What threats have you identified?

By reviewing your SWOT analysis, you will be able to determine where you stack up to the competition. You will also be able to uncover gaps in the market that you can capitalize on.

Don't start working on developing a product like an online course without conducting a competitive analysis. More importantly, don't use this exercise to compare yourself to others. You are unique and bring a special gift to your audience. Use this exercise to differentiate yourself and identify gaps that you can take advantage of.

Now that you have some basic information about your perfect customer, it's time to conduct some research. If you can, interview individuals who are your perfect customer. This can be done via an online survey or a phone interview. Another option is to find an online community like a Facebook group, where your ideal customer hangs out, and ask for feedback in that forum. You will want to tailor the questions for your ideal customer, but here are some examples to get your creative juices flowing:

- What frustrates you about (*insert the problem you are solving*)?
- Have you ever paid to solve this problem?
- How much is it worth to you to get this problem solved?
- What do you think could be improved about (*insert the problem you are solving*)?
- How would you feel if this was solved for you?
- What type of pain does this cause you?
- How much would you pay to solve this problem? (**Hint:** It's important to confirm that your ideal customer will pay money for your online course.)

The biggest ah-ha moment that you are trying to get out of this exercise is your ideal customer's pain point, their migraine. You want to know their problems so you can figure out how to solve them.

Step 4: Craft Your Unique Selling Position

After you've determined who you want to help and how you will help them, the next step is crafting your unique selling position. What do you offer that others in your field do not? This allows you to set yourself apart from the competition and focus on creating courses and offers your perfect customer needs.

It has been said that if you cannot summarize what sets you apart in a few sentences, then you are not unique in your market. I'll give you a specific example from my business.

I have a Facebook and Instagram Ads course. Now, there are a lot of these courses in the market, and many of them are general. However, my course is strictly focused on helping online course creators sell their online courses. Not only that, my unique selling position is that I help them not only fill up their funnel (with leads), but I guide them through how to convert these leads to paying customers.

HOT TIP: The more specific you are in your unique selling position, the more your course will appeal to your ideal customer.

You may be asking; how can I make my online course business unique in a crowded market? Consider these options:

- Provide exceptional support (beyond just a private Facebook group).
- Limit access to X number of people, which promotes exclusivity.
- Give VIP touchpoints, such as bundled-in 1:1 coaching.
- Risk-free guarantee with no "homework" required.

Step 5: Pick the Perfect Business Name

By now, you have the idea for your online course business, an outline of your ideal customer, and how you will differentiate yourself in the marketplace. You may be asking yourself, should I name the business my own personal name or something else? This is an important decision because it influences your social-media account name, setting up your LLC or corporation, and buying a domain name for your website.

Here is some food for thought. Many experts, including online course creators, will name their business their own personal name, and there are many advantages to this. It allows you to pivot over the years. You can add services and products easily, including coaching, additional courses, and speaking engagements.

Key Takeaway and Action Items

Before you move on to the next step, put a stake in the ground on who you intend to serve and your unique selling position on how you will help them. It's ok if you haven't fully fleshed this out. You'll receive clarity with action.

Now, you can move on to the next step, building your audience, so you have someone to help and sell to.

Chapter 4: Building Your Audience

I know from talking to many online course entrepreneurs that the #1 frustration is building their audience. They are not alone. This is a challenge for most entrepreneurs. We don't live in a "build it, and they will come" world. The market is way too crowded. Before any entrepreneur develops their online course program, they should focus first on building their audience.

Why? Your audience will help guide you in what is needed in your program. After all, you don't want to spend time and money creating an online course that no one will buy! You can talk to your audience about their pain points (aka their migraine) and their biggest frustrations.

"People can live with a headache, but they will pay top dollar to get rid of a migraine."

The Author

The good news is that it's not essential to have a large following. In fact, it can be better to have a small group of people who are insanely interested in what you have to offer. Who is your audience? It's not necessarily your Facebook friends, but rather it's the group of people who are likely to buy your online program.

How to Build Your Audience Without a Huge Marketing Budget

A website is a must-have for starting your online course business. While you're just starting out, this can be just a simple website where people can go to get more information about you and how you can help them.

You will have your primary lead magnet on this website, which starting out can be a simple PDF with a video that gives your ideal customer a quick win. Having a lead magnet and a way to collect email addresses is the most important thing you need to do to build your audience. It's more important than starting a Facebook group or your Instagram account.

You will also use your website as a platform for your content management strategy, whether that is blogging or hosting your show notes from your podcast. Your website copy should speak directly to your ideal customer and clearly indicate what you do and your unique selling position discussed in Chapter 3. In other words, your website will showcase why your ideal customer should work with you over your competitor.

Community Group

Using a community group is another opportunity to build your audience and allows your ideal customer to get to know you better by building the know, like, and trust factor. This can be a Facebook group, a Slack group, or even a LinkedIn group. One caveat based on my experience: community groups can be time-consuming to manage, but they offer an excellent opportunity to build your audience and attract future students, especially when you're just starting out.

Another positive for community groups is that they are easy to set up.

You may have some challenges in the beginning finding and attracting your audience, but there are strategies that you can implement to jumpstart this growth. A few examples include joining a few Facebook groups or LinkedIn groups where your ideal customer hangs out. (Be extremely helpful in those groups and invite your ideal customer to join your group via social media and on your website.)

Social Media

You should promote your free lead magnet on social media. There are two ways you can approach this to build your audience. On social media, in your profile, provide links to either: 1) your community group; or 2) your lead magnet. At the end of the day, you want to build your email list and the know, like, and trust factor with your audience. You can do this in both your community group and through email marketing.

Public Relations

Both guest blogging and being a guest on a podcast help establish you as an expert in your field; it can also lead to increased email subscribers, community-group members, and even client bookings! My favorite way to grow my audience is through guest podcast appearances. To find these opportunities and appropriately pitch yourself to the podcast host, you need to have your media page and relevant topics that you feel comfortable speaking about.

Content Marketing

You want your ideal customer to find you through your content management strategy. But how do you develop a content management strategy? Here are some key considerations for your content marketing strategy to help you grow your audience.

Determine your platform for your content

This can be through blogging, podcasting, or videos. My suggestion to start out is to do whatever you feel the most comfortable. If you love to write, then blog. Do you have the gift of gab? Then podcasting may be the best strategy for you. If you are great on video, then you may want to consider a combination of YouTube videos and blogging, also known as a vlog.

Tailor your content for your ideal customer and provide massive value. Once you start interacting with your audience, you will find out precisely what they are struggling with and where they need help. These are the topics you should focus on when producing content.

Produce your content on a consistent basis

In general, it is recommended that you produce content weekly at a minimum. However, keep in mind that you can also repurpose content. Let's say that you are a blogger. But in addition to your blog post, you also do a weekly Facebook Live in your group. You can always repurpose that Facebook Live as a blog post with show notes in a future week.

Distribute and promote your content

Share your content on all the social platforms that apply to your target market. For me, I share my new blog posts and podcasts on Twitter, LinkedIn, Facebook, Instagram, and Pinterest. I get most of my traffic to my website from Pinterest. Because Pinterest functions like a search engine and my pins are shared through my Tailwind Communities (thank you, community members!), Pinterest pins have a long shelf life and can go viral, reaching a large audience.

Use Opt-Ins to Grow Your Email List

Use your content management strategy to grow your email list by creating opt-ins, also known as free gifts. An opt-in is a free giveaway that visitors can sign up for that's directly related to that content, but essentially, they are lead magnets. For instance, let's assume that you wrote a blog post on online course ideas. A possible lead magnet or opt-in for this blog post is a Google sheet that lists 101+ Online Course Ideas. You can place the sign-ups for your opt-in throughout your blog-post content or in your podcast show notes.

Creating Your First Lead Magnet

Here's a pop quiz for you. Out of all the options above, which one is the most important? Where should you start? **Hint:** It's not starting a Facebook group or even setting up your social media accounts. I don't even want you building an expensive website right now or starting a blog or podcast until you've done this.

What's important and the ONE thing you should focus on to build your audience? Setting up a simple landing page where you offer a free gift so you can collect email addresses. It's that simple. To do this, you need a lead magnet (your free gift), a landing-page builder, and an email service provider. Let's start with creating your lead magnet.

Examples of Lead Magnets for Your Online Course

Simply put, a lead magnet is a valuable piece of content that you give to your audience for free in exchange for their name and email address. Your goal is to build your email list. At some point in the future, you may have more than one lead magnet (sometimes referred to as opt-ins, as we mentioned above). For example, when you go to someone's blog post, they may have a special opt-in for that blog post that is different from their main lead magnet on the front page of their website.

In exchange for your free gift, you'll collect their email address. Your call to action on your social media accounts will be to your landing page with your free gift. If you post in a Facebook group on a promotional day, you'll offer up your free gift. Eventually, you'll run Facebook ads to get sign-ups for your free gift.

The goal is for you to start building your email list so you can interact with your audience to understand how you can help them. Your free gift should align with your future online course. Keep in mind that you will most likely not hit the nail on the head in the beginning. You may test out several different lead magnets before you find one that is perfect for your audience and your online course. And this is ok. Now, let's talk about what makes a good lead magnet for your online course.

First, you want your lead magnet to be specific and related to your future online course demonstrating your expertise. The lead magnet will begin to take your prospect on the buyer's journey to show them that YOU can help them solve their problem.

Be sure that you're delivering the free gift right away. This provides immediate gratification, and when it's not sent immediately, people forget what they signed up for.

A Lead Magnet That's Worthy of a Facebook Ad

I don't want you to create just any lead magnet. I want you to create a lead magnet that's worthy of a Facebook ad. There's a difference between a low-value lead magnet and one that delivers true value to the end-user.

Consider this. How many lead magnets have you signed up for in the past and didn't even download them? I'm also a big fan of lead magnets that require the end-user to invest their most valuable asset, which is their time.

When someone is willing to invest time, that means that they are truly interested in what you have to offer and are willing to commit to *solving their problem.* These are what I call future students. They are not freebie-seekers. They are action-takers.

Freebie-seekers are people who are just looking for free stuff. They aren't the ones who'll buy your future course. If you want to stay away from freebie-seekers, consider a lead magnet that's much more than a simple cheat-sheet or checklist. Or you can include a video training to go along with your cheat-sheet or checklist. Examples include:

- Quiz
- Ultimate guides with video
- Email course with video or audio training
- 5-day email challenge or video series
- Mini-workshop series

- Mini-course
- Spreadsheets/calculators with video training
- Toolkits with training videos
- Swipe files with training videos
- Templates with video training
- Planners with video training
- Audio training

If you're still stuck on trying to figure out the best lead magnet for your online course business, go through these steps:

Step 1: Research your industry/competitors. What are they using? (note: you aren't going to copy but use this for inspiration and guidance)

Step 2: Look at examples outside of your industry. Pay attention to Facebook and Instagram ads. What are others using for lead magnets to grow their email list?

Step 3: Sign up for email lists. What does their lead magnet look like?

Step 4: Then ask yourself, what are the top questions you're asked by your ideal customer? What are your ideal customer's biggest pain points (their migraine)? What do they want to accomplish? How can you help them get there? What content could you provide that would knock their socks off so they would say, "I can't believe I just got this for free?"

Just know that you'll likely change lead magnets along the way, the better you get to know your ideal customer and what they need help with. Just get started because clarity comes with action. Now that you have your lead magnet that's worthy of a Facebook ad, let's move on to creating your landing page.

The Landing Page for Your Lead Magnet

This is the website that your prospects will go to sign up for your lead magnet. I highly recommend that you use a landing-page builder for your lead magnet. These pages have been proven to convert, and the last thing you want to happen is to spend money and time driving traffic to your landing page and have people leave without signing up.

There are many different landing-page builders in the market, including Leadpages, Instapage, and Unbounce. Besides, most email service providers like ConvertKit have built-in landing pages that you can use. Some online course platforms are all-in-one platforms like Kajabi. This means that you can host your online course and website on Kajabi. It also handles email, landing pages for your online-course sales funnels, and payment for your online course. You can also have your community hosted on Kajabi rather than Facebook, and they offer an app for your online course. The downside of using Kajabi is that it's a little pricey for someone who's just starting out, but you can save money over the long term and won't have the hassle of integrating various systems later down the road. Kajabi offers top-notch customer support, so if you ever run into any issue or need assistance, they're there for you.

A few things to remember with your landing page. Your call to action should be in the first person. For example, "sign me up," "I want this," or "send it to me now!" Don't forget to include a link (at the bottom) to your privacy policy on your landing page, as this is required if or when you run paid ads. Also, only ask for information that you need, like their email address and first name. You don't need their last name, telephone number, or anything else for your email list.

After someone registers for your lead magnet, you will direct them to your thank you page. This is a simple page that says thank you for signing up and to go check their email for their free gift. Later, you can transform this simple thank-you page into a tripwire offer to turn your subscribers into instant customers.

Set Up Your Email Nurture Sequence

Once your new subscriber is on your email list, the first email you send them will contain their free gift. Then, you'll begin your email nurture sequence. This is also known as a welcome sequence, but the goal is simple: you want to start building the know, like, and trust factor with your new email subscriber. It's also the perfect opportunity for you to interact with your audience and ask them questions.

Your email welcome sequence can be one to two weeks in length. I generally recommend between 5 and 7 emails for your nurture sequence. You will set this up in your email system, so the emails are sent automatically, allowing you to scale. When you're just starting out without an online course to sell (and you're still trying to learn more about your audience), your email sequence will look like this:

Example Email Sequence for a New Online Business

Email #1: Introduction + Lead Magnet Delivery. Send out immediately. In this email, you will introduce yourself, celebrate them for signing up, and send their free gift so they can take immediate action. End the email by letting them know what to expect next.

Email #2: Provide value and another quick win. Send out on Day 2. In this email, provide additional value and give them another quick win. You can also refer back to your lead magnet to help encourage them to take action.

Email #3: Ask a question. Send out 2 days later. Ask them to respond and answer a question. This is your opportunity to get to know your audience and what they may be struggling with.

Email #4: How would you feel if your life looked like [fill in the blank]? Send out 2 days later. In this email, you should talk about their future state (after their problem is solved). Describe how life would feel and look like if only their problem were solved.

Email #5: Encourage a call-to-action. Send out 2 days later. In this email, ask them to take action. This could be setting up a discovery call with you, booking a service, or following you on social media.

Once you create your online course, you will modify this email sequence to invite your prospect to a recorded training where you'll promote your online course or send them directly to a sales page.

Test Your Sales Funnel

Did you notice that I said sales funnel here? While you don't have anything to sell (yet), congratulations, you've just set up a basic online course sales funnel! I want you to test it before it goes live. Enroll just like your ideal customer would sign up for your lead magnet and make sure everything is working correctly, and all your emails are published and ready to go.

Promote Your Lead Magnet

Now the fun begins! Start promoting your lead magnet everywhere. Promote it on all your social media accounts and in Facebook groups on promo days. Your goal is to get sign-ups to your email list. Now, you're all set with your landing page and have a way to capture email addresses and interact with your audience.

Online Course Creator

Story of an Online Course Creator's Journey

Jodi Bourne

Jodi Bourne helps vacation rental owners and property managers market their vacation rentals directly to guests without using sites like Airbnb. She is a Web designer, Course Creator, and Consulting Coach in the travel and tourism industry. She has completed over 10 websites, has tons of clients, and her Instagram course has been a great resource to her market.

Website is https://jodibourne.com and @heyjodibourne on Instagram

Like many women today, Jodi had children first, then went back to college and started her career in her late 30s. She began working in the non-profit human services sector, specifically domestic violence against women. After 4 years of experiencing so much sadness and burnt-out, she needed a change. Her daughter had some health issues, and the daily 9-to-5 grind was making it difficult to schedule time off. She needed to find a flexible job to balance the demands of both her personal and professional life. Lucky to have some financial support at the time, she decided to start her own freelancing business from home. This way, she could build her business a little at a time, be there for her daughter, and have the ability to finally do something fun and exciting.

The local music scene was thriving in her area of Texas, so she started to work with local musicians, marketing music venues, and connecting with local businesses. Her involvement with the small-town convention visitor bureau (CVB) introduced her to different facets of entertainment, hospitality, as well as the growing tourism industry, specifically in Austin, Texas. Working with the CVB expanded her business and spurred her interest in the travel and tourism industry. It was exciting and super-fun.

At the same time, her interest in tourism was evolving. She began working part-time as a freelancer with a course creator who showed her the ropes beyond the scope of traditional marketing. This course creator optimized courses for other people, working with many industry leaders through digital marketing. During this period, people were beginning to create their own websites, which led her to discover that anyone could build a website and use it for their business. However, many businesses were not actually using their websites to their advantage or to what she considered "a portal to their customer base."

She started working with hotels, vacation rental owners, and property management companies outside the Austin area. Networking with individual owners, she discussed with them building a Book to Direct Business. Little did she know this movement was growing across the country. People were getting tired of booking on VRBO, Home Away, Bookings.com, and Airbnb. People were tired of being charged a hefty fee for simply booking a rental. A 12 to 15% fee goes to VRBO from the renter; in addition, the property owners have to pay a fee for the service as well, between 12 and 15%. This 24 to 30% total increase presented difficulties for some business owners. If customers could avoid using these services and instead have a way of booking directly, it would result in huge, significant savings. It would also save money for the owners and reduce the overall rental rate of the property.

There are steps to direct booking s. The first step is creating a website with a booking platform. People go to the website, review the property, and then book the property and pay. This ability to book directly allows the guest to communicate before and after the booking. The website is set up with a contact and phone number and a method of booking the property out, method of payment, minus the 30% for a third-party internet booking service. A win for both the customer and rental owner.

Systems, such as Airbnb, VRBO, HomeAway, and others that book properties through their internet booking systems have many downfalls. For one, the customer doesn't get to communicate directly with the owner or the property manager. The customer is paying an extra fee to book the rental, and the owner/property manager is paying or passing the cost on to the customer for this service. People who are booking directly are interested in the details of their stay, what activities are available in the area, and so on. Owners/property managers are just as interested in their guest experience and making sure they can secure repeat bookings. Direct bookings are a win-win. The focus was on vacation rental owners and property managers, building their websites, social media presence, and assisting them with branding their online business.

Jodi initially started out helping businesses with their social media, but she saw a pattern of why her customers' social media was not gaining the traction needed to be profitable. You see, the websites of many of her customers, who set up their direct bookings on their sites, did not have their sites working properly. In fact, many of the sites were DIY created in-house, often outdated, had poor pictures of their rental, the booking integration didn't work properly, no analytics were set up on the system, and they were not mobile-friendly. Their customer base portal was more like a black hole to nowhere than a portal to the vacation dream rental. This is what led her to create websites for her customers.

Having had the experience in 2015 working with the course creator, Jodi was very familiar with working with industry leaders, helping them optimize their courses and build their sales funnels to integrate into their online businesses. She did some work with a client named Digital Marketer and worked with Webinar Jam, which was one of the original webinar systems where you could get people to take over a webinar for free or pay them. Wanting to build her knowledge in website creation, she spent $2,000 taking a WordPress course and learned how to build websites.

Working freelance gave her the ability to learn about course creating and what industry leaders were looking for. She quickly learned how to build courses and built her first one in 2018. Back then, none of the Instagram courses talked about the travel industry or tourism. So, she found the perfect niche to create her course. Her first course was an Instagram course with a focus on tourism. This course was unique, unlike any of the typical courses on Instagram at the time, because it focused on the travel and tourism industry, vacations, rental owners, and small hotels. Since then, she has added many more courses to her program and built a very successful business.

Starting out on the service side allowed her to connect with her audience and establish a niche market. It provided great information about her ideal market, what the needs of her audience would be, and how she would help them. She was able to clearly identify the customer base she was serving, the pain points of her perfect ICAs, acknowledge age demographics, and often, their lack of tech knowledge. She knew her market and had an overall understanding of the business she loved. This start as a service provider led to her growth as a successful course creator.

Some of her beginning missteps in creating her online business were her lack of a set-up and a working sales funnel. She had conducted a podcast with a vacation rental expert, which in return directed traffic to their site. She made a very common mistake of thinking that everyone would listen to her podcast and immediately connect to her link and buy her course. The only problem was she didn't have the ability to get them on an email list and move them towards a purchase. She had a sales funnel, but it was not on her front page, like a splash page on a website. She was doing Facebook ads and leading people to her Instagram course; however, she didn't have her sales funnel set up on her homepage.

While she had a lead magnet set up, which was a guide for using Instagram for the tourism industry, and she was proud of her five-page guide, she made the mistake of thinking that people would actually go to the website or the link. Instead, they Google searched her name and then came to the home page. They downloaded the lead magnet, which sent them to the sales page, giving them access to the very first video of her course. This was a general overview of Instagram and how to use it for this industry. They then could either buy from the sales page, and if they didn't, she would walk them through a three-email sales funnel, where she would try to convince them to buy the course. If people decided not to buy, she would move them to the smaller sales funnel, a webinar funnel where she did a one-hour mini-course.

This process made her realize that her steps were not working. In part, because most people in the industry, by the time they have a vacation rental or vacation rental business, have already made a hefty investment. She found that many were in their early to late fifties or older and were new to all the technology. She quickly realized that they needed help creating a profile, assistance on adding images, and really overwhelmed with the technology part. The conclusion was that perhaps her initial offering was too complicated and needed to be simplified. She asked for feedback and began consulting using teaching strategies that would give them immediate results. Talking to her people and finding out what they really needed, looking at the data, and making tweaks along the way helped her recreate her offerings.

So, teaching the basics led to how they actually get bookings. This turned into additional modules being added and different techniques to teach in order to get bookings. It also helped her set up a group coaching course and add live coaching as part of her business. A good amount of her revenue comes from building websites for vacation rental property owners, and she is booked months out. She also utilizes her experience and knowledge of her audience's pain points to create courses, offer group and live coaching, create copy, set up social-media services, blog, and for content marketing. This approach helps guide her customers through the necessary steps to help them brand their businesses.

She has devoted much time to service, getting to know her customers, and helping them create the perfect sales experience for their businesses. This is done by the listing description of their property, sometimes helping them rename their rentals or their business, as well as the social media set-up services that are required. She had found that social-media management was difficult to offer with so many different destinations, the expense for the client to pay to have research conducted, and learn all the ins and outs of those destinations. Each place is in a different location, so what she has been successful at is teaching them how to manage and navigate their business into a profitable one and get them off the listing sites and into direct bookings. She achieves this goal by offering coaching consulting, also known as rental-specific services.

One of her favorite things to do is offer blogging. The content marketing aspect of learning about areas, researching, keyword search, and blogging for her clients is second to her website services. She has created a following of people looking to learn the ins and outs of the tourism industry, particularly the direct movement. This part of her business will continue to grow as she walks people through the step-by-step process.

Having the group consulting serves clients that have just one or two properties and can't afford the one-on-one coaching experience, which is an eight-week course where she teaches them directly and gives them access to videos. They also get access to this course information to use later on if they need to refer back to anything.

Perhaps the most motivating part of Jodi's story is that she is passionate about what she does. She provides a service in an industry she loves, helping people learn how to run their online businesses. In 2021, she plans to add to her mini-courses, email marketing, blogging, Instagram, Facebook group, and a marketing course as well as a Pinterest course. She will continue to grow her group coaching courses. She has 2 different ICAs, which consist of small property management companies, and the second type, luxury properties and vacation rental investors, who have a large portfolio of properties. The difference is the amount of rental income generated by both types.

Her advice for course creators:

"You can't without a lead magnet. You definitely have to have something on your website that generates leads that you can put into an email system and follow up with people on. It is the best way to get those customers. Even if you're getting people that aren't interested in your services, you're learning something about them just by seeing which lead magnets they download."

"There is no such thing as failure in marketing. When you fail, you've learned, learned how to implement better strategies and how to optimize your own marketing."

Key Takeaway and Action Items

Creating your lead magnet and setting up a way to collect email addresses is the most important action item to focus on for your online course business. If you don't do anything else in this chapter, focus on this.

Chapter 5: Discover Your Profitable Course Idea

Many new entrepreneurs get stuck when it comes to picking their first online course idea. I get this. You want to find the perfect course and can't afford to waste any time on a project that doesn't yield results. You can spend hours and hours brainstorming course topics and content only to find out that there is a course out there on the same topic. Even worse, you worry about creating a course that no one buys after you have put all that time, energy, and marketing dollars into it.

The good news is that if there is a course on the market already covering your exact topic, there is a market for what you want to teach, and people are willing to pay for it.

Remember that competition validates market demand.

"Competition for your online course topic validates market

demand."

I will walk you through my 4-step system, which will help you discover and validate your course idea so you can move forward with your revenue-generating course today. But, before I do that, let's cover the different types of courses you can create.

Option 1: Mini-Course

A mini-course, also known as a tiny product or starter course, would be considered a no-brainer type of offer . An offer that you could sell immediately from a Facebook ad and your target market would see the ad and think, "I can't live without this," and click to buy.

These offers are generally quite low in price and are usually between $27-$47 for the business market and $7 - $17 for the consumer market.

How a Mini-Course Can Be Successful

Once someone clicks to buy, there's an order bump offered that may be priced even a little higher, like a workshop at $97. And then "wait!" before they finish the checkout process, another offer is presented that may even be a little higher, like another course at $197.

In this scenario, the total purchase price may end up being around $321, depending on how many products the customer purchased. For this to work, you need to have several products to offer and a top-notch marketing system with strong Facebook ad knowledge. This system requires you to run Facebook ads to continue to find people (a cold audience) that would be interested in your mini-course (aka tiny offer).

Additionally, when you run a Facebook ad campaign for an offer such as this, you'll likely see a higher ROI initially in the ad campaign, and, after some time, you'll start to see lower conversion rates as you saturate the market.

Now, don't get me wrong, I love what I call self-liquidating type funnels, where I run Facebook ads either directly to a low-cost digital product or a free offer with a tripwire to a low-cost digital product.

They help pay or even fully fund my Facebook ads, but most importantly, I have an instant customer.

One that I can upsell to my higher-end services or products.

Here's why I love a mini-course:

- They allow you to gain the momentum to get started. So many course creators get stuck in the analysis-paralysis mode.
- It's easier to create than a high-end premium offer.
- When used as a tripwire, you can gain an instant customer with a mini-course.
- With a mini-course, you can use it to help fund or even cover your ad costs.
- A mini-course can be used as a gateway so you can upsell your services or future courses.
- A mini-course serves as a starting point for the buyer's journey and gives them just a taste of what it's like to work with

you.

- A mini-course can serve as a beta (test) course for your future signature program.

You will not stop with just creating just a mini-course, and here's why. You want to take your students on a journey and allow them the opportunity to continue to learn and work with you. Here are some other options and courses to consider as you continue to build out your product portfolio:

- A signature course
- A subject-matter course

Let's talk about the differences between these two options.

Option 2: A Signature Course

A signature course is more like a degree program, similar to getting your MBA. It's a premium course that may even have some coaching or other support options bundled in with it. It's a comprehensive, end-to-end framework so that when your students complete it, they've experienced a complete transformation.

Option 3: A Subject-Matter Course

A subject-matter course, on the other hand, would be like taking a course in a degree program. You delve deep into that subject matter to help your students master that specific content, whether it is learning a type of software or mastering a part of what you may touch upon in your signature program.

Let's take some specific examples from my business.

An example of a mini-course that I previously offered is an Ad Starter Kit. This mini-course was used as a tripwire and led into my "Subject Matter Course," the Funnel Fill-Up & Convert Formula, where I helped online business owners fill up their funnel using Facebook and Instagram ads and convert them to paying customers.

An example of a signature course would be a program where I help entrepreneurs both create and launch their online courses into the market, including setting up their online course sales funnels and launching with a webinar or 5-day challenge. As you can see, this type of signature course would be a total transformation for my students.

What Type of Course Should I Create First?

I'm a big fan of mini-courses. They can be used as tripwires for when you start running Facebook ads, which is a tool to gain an instant customer and self-fund your ads at the same time. It's also easier to get started with a mini-course, so if you're just dipping your toes into creating your first online course, consider creating a mini-course.

In my online course business and some of my peers' enterprises, mini-course are used to grow your email list with your perfect students while at the same time recovering some (or all) ad costs. Just know that if you start with a mini-course , to serve your audience and sustain your business in the long term, you will likely need future courses in your portfolio.

Mini-courses help your students get started. For example, in my own business, I focus on helping online course business owners sell their online courses using online sales funnels and Facebook and Instagram ads.

However, I found that many people who were coming to me to run Facebook ads needed help with creating a lead magnet worthy of a Facebook ad. So, I decided to create a mini-course to help them with this step.

Another example in my business is my Ad Copy Toolbox. This is a mini-course that walks you through exactly what to say in your Facebook ad copy with plug-n-play templates and swipe files so you can start converting your visitors even before they click on your landing page. This mini-course feeds into other programs like my Ad Starter Kit and my Funnel Fill-Up & Convert program, which is an in-depth course designed for online course creators in filling up their webinar, 5-day challenge, or summit with Facebook and Instagram Ads to sell their online course.

In the two examples I provided

above, because my students wanted to run a list-building Facebook ad but didn't have a lead magnet that would work for an ad campaign, my *Magic Attraction* mini-course was a perfect tiny offer.

In my other example, my students wanted to dip their toes in Facebook ads but didn't know where to start. The Ad Copy Toolbox and Ad Starter Kit examples are perfect for them to walk through exactly how to create their first ad campaign.

How to Discover Your Profitable Course Idea

To discover your profitable course idea, think about what you could offer to kick start your students' momentum. If you're stuck at any time during this process, think about this question: **What's keeping my students from moving forward?**

To come up with possible course ideas, first start by reviewing your passion, skills, and achievements. If you are a coach or consultant, think about what aspects of your current role would translate to an online course. If you are a service professional, consider if you could supplement any part of your current service with an online program. Do you have a special skill set where you could teach others? What is your superpower?

Next, talk with your customers or your social media following. Ask them if they would pay for an online training if you offered it. Do you have a certification that you offer in your consulting line of work? This is an excellent opportunity to put your content in an online course with a digital badging program. Or perhaps an online course would allow you to expand and help customers that you aren't serving today due to geographical limitations or other reasons. Anything goes here! List any course idea that may be viable for your business that fits your skillset and passion. If you're looking for some additional inspiration, here are some sites and places to go for ideas about your course:

- Online course sites, such as Udemy, Brit + Co, Skillshare, and Lynda.com.

- Search for Facebook groups or LinkedIn groups in your niche. Spend some time in the groups to see what kind of questions people ask related to your area of expertise.
- Amazon is a great online research tool and will show you hot topics related to books, which can translate into an online course.
- Your good friend Google. Google trends and just searching on Google will give you some great insight into what's popular and in-demand related to your area of expertise. Search for your area of expertise (e.g., how to eat vegan) + course and see what you find.

Course Creators
Story of an Online Course
Creator's Journey
Stacey Juba

Stacey Juba is a writer as well as a freelance developmental editor, creator of online courses for writers, and an award-winning journalist, who has published more than 3,000 articles in newspapers and magazines. She is the author of the *Storybook Valley* chick-lit series, the *Hockey Rivals Sports* series for young adults, and many more. She is the founder of "Shortcuts for Writers." Her signature course, "Editing Blueprint," is a step-by-step plan that empowers fiction writers to think like an editor so they can save time and money. Stacey's books are located at https://stacyjuba.com, and her courses and editing can be found on https://shortcutsforwriters.com where there is also a link to her Facebook group.

Stacey published her first novel when she was 18 years old. Her first book was successful, but like most writers, it wasn't a continuous stream of good fortune, and she had several years of rejection. She continued to write her books on the side while working at a newspaper as a journalist. After having kids, she worked from home doing freelance work with companies like *Parenting Magazine* and then branched out into editing newsletters. At the time, a lot of her beginning writings focused on health and fitness articles. Through some traditional publishers, small presses, and even indie publishers, she had several more of her books published. She built up a lot of experience and started doing developmental editing work with fiction and non-fiction writers in various genres.

There are many different types of editors, such as developmental editors, line editors, copy editors, and proofreaders. Her focus was on developmental and line editing. Developmental editing is like giving a broad overview of the whole book. So, for fiction, it would be looking at the characters, the character development, the plot, the pacing, the dialogue, the technique, and the word choice. For non-fiction, it would be a similar structure, but more about how the subject is presented and its flow. The line editing usually occurs when a writer is further along in the process when the manuscript is almost complete. If a manuscript needs a lot of significant structural changes and lots of extensive rewrites, then a writer would want to focus on those first. Especially when doing rewrites, because if you start working on the line editing, all those little changes could become obsolete. Line editing is looking at the sentences, tightening them up, making them flow better, changing some of the word choices. Copy editors focus on grammar, punctuation, continuity, and small details. Also, for a non-fiction book, copy editors might verify facts, look for vague or ambiguous sentences, and things of that nature.

Stacey had a few regular clients for her freelance newsletters, but then many of them started to do their newsletters in-house. She was now looking for a way to fill the gap in her income. At this time, self-publishing was really taking off, and things like Kindle and Nook had just hit the market. Many opportunities were starting to open up for authors. Before this time, in the early 1990s, self-publishing required a large upfront investment of money. You would have to buy hundreds of copies of your book and market them yourself. Whereas now print-on-demand is available for the print versions, and then, of course, there are the e-book versions.

It was an optimal time for freelancers in many different aspects of publishing and just as many opportunities for various kinds of editors, formatters, and cover designers. So, Stacey decided to venture into editing, and she did really well. She started building her client lists and getting testimonials. She noticed that there was a common misconception that beginner writers seemed to have. They didn't realize how the editing process worked and would often start with the wrong type of editor. Editing is an expensive part of the process, and most authors need multiple rounds of editing before their book is completed. They also don't realize all the structural issues that the manuscript might have. For many, unfortunately, it doesn't register until they have published their book and start receiving negative reviews on Amazon or rejections from agents and publishers. Many authors underestimate the editing process and don't realize how expensive it is. When they do hire a freelance editor, they often hire the wrong kind or hire way too early, when what they have is essentially only a rough draft. Most beginner writers will need at least four rounds of developmental editing.

Stacey began to see that in some circumstances, she was privately teaching the craft of writing. She also realized that if some writers needed more than four rounds of editing, it would amount to hundreds of dollars, which most of her customers couldn't afford. With this in mind, she began to see that a lot of editors and a lot of authors needed a go-to guide when working with an editor. This is when she started thinking about becoming an online course creator. She wanted to create a course that would be a prerequisite for writers on when to hire an editor. Once they were provided with a guide, they would be able to do a lot of self-editing on their own. This would help them bring their manuscript up to a higher level before they actually started putting money into their book.

Around 2012 was the time when self-publishing really took off, and there was a great demand in the marketplace. Having young children at the time, Stacey realized that there were limits to how many clients she could take on. She also realized that there was only so much editing she could do in a week and had to limit herself to one or two books a month when her kids were in school. Editing also required a tremendous amount of time and creative energy, and she was beginning to feel burned out. She needed to find some balance. Perhaps the breaking point came for her one year when she took a hard look at her taxes and profit margin. She realized she wasn't making the amount of money she should have been. Between her expenses, taxes, and the amount of time she was putting in, she was disappointed.

After having worked with so many clients in so many different genres, she began to discover that they were all making the same types of mistakes. She even created a Word file where she would paste just general information, tracking those types of mistakes. Among the many mistakes were authors telling rather than showing, using commonly overused words, or using too many words to make their point. Regardless of what genre it was, whether it was a mystery, a romance, a time-travel book, or a non-fiction book, she was just seeing very similar mistakes. This is when she realized that she could create a course that would be a mutually beneficial product for both writers and editors. To scale her business, work with more clients without burning herself out, and provide a mutually beneficial product, she began to map out the type of course she was going to create.

By 2017, Stacey was testing the waters. She started to take many free webinars on online course creation, learning about funnels and the different "Teachable" versus "Thinkific" platforms available. The next several months were spent on research and learning. Around 2018, she bought the Devi software and began what would be a long process of building her course. She had her website Stacyjuba.com, but that site was for her books. Wanting to simplify her offerings without confusing her audience, she developed a new website specifically for her editing and online courses.

There was so much to learn from technology, making videos, audio, and everything else involved, and she was determined to meet her goals. She also was taking the steps that all successful entrepreneurs take; she was educating herself on every aspect of her business, including defining her objectives, reviewing her branding, outlining her market strategy, the sales funnels, the lead magnets, and everything that is required to set up a successful online course business.

She launched her Facebook group in the spring of 2019 and then launched her online course in March 2020. The pandemic and all the lockdowns started when she was right in the middle of her sales funnel. It wasn't the ideal time to launch; however, she still did well. She met the challenge head-on, developed the prelaunch and then her first launch. She developed a lead magnet for her line-editing course, created her editing course, focused on publicizing the course and getting people on her email list. She friended other writers on Facebook and sent them invitations to her group. In addition, she sought out different writers' groups where promotion is allowed on certain days and advertised the launch of her course. She created a prelaunch phase and wrote blog posts sharing her personal story of how she had been overwhelmed by editing in the past and the importance of writers understanding the process and different aspects of editing.

Even more impressive, Stacey created a trailer for her course and uploaded it to YouTube. She made videos allowing prospective customers to take a tour now followed by a sample lesson. She also knew it would benefit her to go live and started with prerecorded videos, then built up the courage to do live videos through her group on Facebook. A successful strategy used was weekly emails in a sequence to her launch, hitting on pain points that gave her customers an understanding of why taking this course would help them and why they needed to take her class.

Many new writers didn't realize what the editing process would entail. Having had collected past email templates, she used some of these to explain the process and the steps of editing, as well as the costs involved. She also had some slides she used from the Editorial Freelancers Association, showing the different costs of editors, the different types of editors, and the average costs. Besides, she added an example of what a developmental editor charges per hour and what they provided for those fees, showing her audience details of the editing process, what to expect, and the fees charged to help them navigate the process.

She focused on educating her audience in her blog posts, videos, and email sequences. Included for a limited time, she added a sale and some bonuses. She did her homework and contacted other service providers, like cover and website designers. They helped her come up with different bonuses, like cheat-sheets for working with a cover designer, or thinking of a cover concept, or what to include on your author website. She had many bonuses placed on a private password-protected page, so if you bought during that period or joined within two weeks, you would get access to that bonus. Sending reminder emails toward the end of the sale, she discovered that what she heard was actually true: a lot of people tend to buy either right at the beginning or the end of a sale. So, she made sure to add a couple of reminder emails on that last day and posted reminders on social media. She found that having a deadline was an important part of the sales cycle because when people saw a deadline, a lot of the sales would happen.

It's important with a launch to have a cart open and cart close date that forces the buyer to make a decision. It's also crucial to build an audience before you launch. This way, you have someone to sell to. Networking on your social media platforms and your Facebook group promotes your sale, making sure you went to all the right places to generate excitement for your product. Stacey, really capitalized on her audience by going to her writer groups and promoting her lead magnet.

The course she was offering was an email course. She started a Trello board where she pasted her course information, so it was available when she started working on marketing the course. She had these templates stored into Trello (a collaboration tool that organizes your projects into boards). She set it up so that she could launch a five-day email course that would eventually transition them into her sales funnel for a paid course. So, basically, it was a five-day course where they get emails delivered to their inbox every day, along with a couple of introductory emails. She then offered a bonus that was like a cheat-sheet, at the end of everything they learned.

She incorporated this into her Facebook group as well. She used the units where people who were taking her line-editing class could go and post their homework. She might provide them with a sentence to revise, like a before and after. They could post it into the unit and then get feedback from the other students in the class. She got a lot of great feedback from this process, and it reinforced what she was teaching. For some of the beginner writers, she would have a lesson where they had to count how many times they used a certain word in their writings. For example: How many times were you using the word "look," and how many times were you using the word "I?" If you write fiction, for example, many people use those words a lot. Too much, in fact! When the writers see these small things pointed out, they can't believe it. Teaching them this one small thing can have a significant impact on their writing. It is also something they can be easily fixed, and with this exercise, you just made them more aware of things that they should work on. The goal is to help them become better writers and to save them time and money. It was an actionable lesson that could make them feel like their writing was improving.

She also added a free book blurb toolkit that directed people to her Facebook group that she used for promotions. This would be, for example: If you become a member of the Facebook Group, you can go to the unit section, and then there's a free book blurb toolkit, which kind of guided them through writing their back-cover copy or the product descriptions you see on Amazon. It had an online flow to it and would take them through a hunt on Amazon. Here, they could find other books in their genre and hone in on approaches that other successful authors use. Providing free resources that were simple enough for students to start using immediately helped to warm them up to purchasing the full class.

When she first launched her course, she was going to sell the course at the regular price, which was $197. And then the launch price was $129, plus they would get access to limited-time bonuses. So, she did have a lot of people join and made close to $5,000 on that launch. It wasn't as much as she had hoped for. At the time, she had about 300 to 400 writers on her email list, and her Facebook group had about 600 to 700 members. For the audience she had and considering that the course was launched in the middle of a pandemic, she felt it was a successful endeavor. She did end up extending the price for a couple of weeks. Some people were appreciative as they were so distracted by all the shutdowns and the pandemic news. As people were home, they realized they wanted something to do, so she extended the closed-cart date.

She also launched another class in early December called the "Energize Your Writing Toolkit, Cheat Sheets for Character Emotions." This was something she had been working on for a while; there was just so much work going into all the marketing of the book. It's a 100-page PDF that she created that focuses on nonverbal communication and body language. A lot of writers tend to use the same body language or nonverbal communication phrases, like "she walked across the room" or "he smiled" or "she glared at him." She broke it down into different emotions and came up with fresh ways to say this and liven up the emotion in their main script. She also created a couple of videos to go with the course and some short assignments. So, it's a combination of an e-book and a mini-course. Launched in December 2020, it did really well.

She's on some different Facebook groups, like a mom to mompreneur. These kinds of Facebook groups have different collaboration threads. So, she would post about having an affiliate program if anybody worked with writers. She had some people approach her who handled other aspects of author services and were interested in being affiliates. And then, periodically, she would do a few podcasts and YouTube shows. Those hosts were creativity coaches or writers themselves or had writing coaches, and many became affiliates.

She has a Trello board of people she has begun to network with. It started with her following them on Instagram or Facebook and getting to know more about them. Sometimes she would send out an email telling them about her program and seeing if they were interested in becoming an affiliate. She hasn't done too many cold calls or emails yet, because she's had too many other things to focus on, but that is one of her priorities for 2021. She's just starting to build up her partnerships and her affiliates and offering a 50% commission. So, it's definitely a huge bonus and incentive for them. There are many different avenues still to explore like, small presses, author groups from other service providers, or proofreaders, copy editors, or people who don't do the same kind of editing that she does.

Stacey is always looking for a mutually beneficial relationship that she can work with and make more connections. She also wants to keep building her Facebook group. She's working on a deadline funnel right now and is in the process of testing it out, having a deadline. In theory, every day, she would be launching a book-editing blueprint to a new group of people who've gone through her line-editing class. And then she has a tripwire, her "Energize your Writing Toolkit." She still has to set up as a tripwire on her site, so once they sign up for her line-editing class, they'll get a timer where they can get their toolkit at a discount for like 20 minutes. She's still testing it out to see how that works, but just trying different things and seeing what seems to work best.

Having a Facebook group has really been effective for her and just building upon her engagement in that group. Again, she started it before she had something to promote so that they don't just associate her with trying to sell them something. She has weekly prompts, like a motivational Monday where they can post their goals for the week, and then a weekend wins prompt, where they share something they're proud of, or they can share a link to their book. She then uses a post-planner as a scheduling tool where she just schedules every few months when she finds a bunch of interesting articles or blog posts on other sites that she thinks would be of interest to them. And then she would just schedule them so that she'd have a couple of posts per week. That way, she's not constantly trying to focus on finding things to post about; it's automatic, and then she can really focus on engaging with them in the comments.

She has noticed that when she posts videos in the group, especially live videos, she'll see a correlation to the people joining her email lists on that day or, shortly afterward, or she'll see increasing sales. If you're nervous about doing videos and Facebook live, this should be something you may focus on mastering. That's something she's had to focus on getting over. It was very intimidating to her, but she definitely saw an increase in sales when she did videos. It's just batching a lot of video ideas and YouTube ideas, having a good lead magnet, having something that's really relevant to you, knowing who your audience is, and knowing what their pain points are.

Key Takeaway and Action Items

You learned that a mini-course is a great way to get started in building your online course business. It allows your ideal students to get to know you and your teaching style. Mini-courses serve as a building block for future subject-matter or signature online courses. Your mini-course can serve as your minimum viable product and allow you to build upon your future online course offering while generating revenue for your business.

Chapter 6: Create Your Online Course

In this chapter, I will walk you through all the steps to create your online course. We will cover how to create your online course outline, build your online course lesson slides and supplemental materials like your workbooks, tips for recording your videos, and selecting your online course platform. Let's get started with Step 1.

Step 1: Create Your Online Course Outline

This step is action-oriented, so get a piece of paper and a pen or a Google Docs sheet before you start. At the top of your paper, outline your promised transformation. This is the result that your students will accomplish after completing your course.

For example, in *Magic Attraction*, the promised transformation is that my students will create a lead magnet that's worthy of a Facebook ad so they can attract action-takers and not freebie-seekers.

Next, I want you to brainstorm content ideas for your course. It's important to keep in mind that you're creating a mini-course. You should be laser-focused on one topic and your promised transformation.

This is not the time to teach them everything you know. It'll overwhelm your students and affect their success. For instance, most of my mini-courses are only three to five lessons.

In addition to the lessons, I have supplemental resources like workbooks, checklists, or cheat-sheets. I may also have sections that include a tech library or how-to resources.

I also recommend you brainstorm what bonus material you can include to help sell your mini-course. Bonuses are great selling features, but keep in mind that bonuses should not be required to achieve your promised transformation. They are above-and-beyond resources that help your audience take their learning to the next level. For example, in my *Magic Attraction* mini-course, I have several bonuses:

1. 231+ High Converting Email Subject Lines: Never get stuck again on what you should write for a subject line so your subscribers will open your email!
2. 7 Ways to Grow Your Email List (Without Spending a Dime): Grow your email list with engaged subscribers every single day with these seven strategies that won't cost you a dime.
3. How To Create a Tripwire and Gain Instant Customers: Learn how you can create a low-cost digital product to turn subscribers into instant customers, so they're primed for your online course launch.

These bonuses help my students achieve some fantastic results, but if I didn't include this content in the mini-course, they would still achieve the transformation I promised them.

Mini-Course Outline

A simple way to create your course outline for a mini-course looks like this:

Promised Transformation: List your promised transformation here:

Course Outline

Lesson 1: Topic

- Supplemental resource (e.g., workbook, cheat-sheet, or checklist)

Lesson 2: Topic

- Supplemental resource (e.g., workbook, cheat-sheet, or checklist)

Lesson 3: Topic

- Supplemental resource (e.g., workbook, cheat-sheet, or checklist)

Lesson 4: Topic

- Supplemental resource (e.g., workbook, cheat-sheet ,or checklist)

Lesson 5: Topic

- Supplemental resource (e.g., workbook, cheat-sheet, or checklist)

Additional Resources (if applicable)

- List any additional resources here

• List any additional resources here
Bonuses!

1 List Bonus #1 here
2 List Bonus #2 here
3 List Bonus #3 here

Now that you have your outline for your course, let's move on to the next step creating your online course lesson slides.

Step 2: Create Your Online Course Teaching Content

In this step, we're focused on creating the content for your online course. This is your teaching content. Think of it like this. In school, your teacher will teach the content. They may do this by speaking in front of the classroom or presenting important information and walking you through the presentation slides. In addition to this content, you may have supplemental materials like a workbook so you can retain what you learned.

Your online course is no

different; you'll have videos where you are teaching the important information your students need and additional materials to help them learn.

Online Course Lesson Slides

The tools used to create your online course lesson slides depend on how you are delivering your course content. You have several options here. You can build your content on slides, such as Canva, PowerPoint, or Keynote, and then record your voice-over. I like to create my online course lessons in Canva. There is a notes section in Canva that you may use as speaker notes, which serves as a teleprompter when recording your course lesson videos.

Another option, which is popular if you are doing a software demo for your course, for example, if you were teaching how to use Excel, is to do a screen recording of your computer. The third option is to record directly to the camera. In this option, you are speaking directly into the camera, teaching your course content. Some course creators do a combination of recording from slides and directly to the camera, but unless you're skilled in editing videos, this can be more difficult to produce. If you need help creating your online course lesson slides, I have an online course lesson template to help you get started in my *Course in a Box* program.

Supplemental Materials

It's important to make your course actionable and provide your students with cheat-sheets, workbooks, how-to guides, and other material so they can take action on the information you have taught them. My recommended go-to tool for creating workbooks, cheat-sheets, and checklists for your online course is Canva. You can create these high-value supplemental resources without hiring a pricey designer and provide them editable materials that increase the value of your online course.

In my *Course in a Box* program,

I've made it easy for online course creators like you to create their supplemental material with templates and training.

Tips for Your Online Course Lessons

If you're teaching how to use software or apps, in this step, you will outline exactly what you will cover in your screen share when you record. This will allow you to create a concise and clear lesson recording in our next step.

If you're new to building presentations, I recommend that you start with Canva. You can design a beautiful and engaging presentation in Canva with their free account. You can create your lesson presentation in Canva and use this to record your course videos with your voice-over.

You don't have to be a designer to use Canva for your course slides. In fact, with the template I've provided in my *Course in a Box* program, you can just plug in your content, modify for your branding, and you're good to go!

Step 3: Record Your Lesson Videos

When you're ready to record your course videos, here are the tools you'll need:

1. Your presentation slides

2. Microphone

3. Webcam (if you want to record a face to camera video)

4. Zoom or Canva (if your presentation slides were created in Canva)

For your microphone, I recommend a Blue Snowball. You can get studio-quality audio, and I even use it for my podcast recordings.

Step 4: Select Your Hosting Option and Upload Course Content

A big question you probably have is: Where should I host my online course content? It's a very valid question, and the answer depends on what you're trying to achieve. First, let's talk about what options are available for course creators. There are three primary ways for course creators to offer their online courses to their students. One is through an online course marketplace, and another is to host your course on an online course platform. The last option is to host your course on your own website with a plug-in. Before we look at the various options for hosting your online course, let me emphasize this:

"The success of your business is NOT dependent upon your online course platform."

– The Author

Let's say that you select a platform below and decide that you want to migrate to a different one in the future. You can do this. I've seen many successful online course creators with thousands of students easily migrate their business to a new platform. Do not let this step stop you from moving forward in launching your business.

Online Course Marketplace

You may ask: What's a course marketplace? The good news is, you're probably already familiar with some of them. Here are some examples:

Udemy

Udemy is one of the most popular online course marketplaces, and they have made it very easy to get started in building your Udemy course by creating your instructor account. They have specific guidelines for course creation, which all instructors are required to abide by. Their course prices target individual consumers, and some cost as little as $15. Instructor pay is based on a revenue-share model.

LinkedIn Learning

LinkedIn Learning is another online course marketplace. You must receive approval to become a LinkedIn Learning instructor, and you are required to send in a sample video so they can get a feel for your teaching style and presentation. Other online course marketplaces include Skillshare, Simplilearn, and Brit + Co.

Pros and Cons of an Online Course Marketplace

The benefit of launching your course on a marketplace is that, for the most part, all marketing is done by the marketplace provider. It's also a good way to validate a course idea and to build awareness around your course. The cons of launching your course on a marketplace platform include:

- Little to no control over the course price, which could dilute the value of your offering in the market and lower your profit margin.
- Instead of the course being associated with your brand name, it is marketed and branded by the marketplace provider.
- You have no access to your customer list or emails, which does not allow you to market to them in the future.
- Often, there are strict guidelines for course publishing.

Not thrilled about using a course marketplace? The good news is you have other options available to you.

Online Course Platform

My favorite option for hosting your

content for your online course is using an online course platform. There are many different options for you to choose from, but here are some of the best solutions:

- Thinkific
- Kajabi
- Teachable
- Podia
- ThriveCart Learn

While I'm not going to go into the specifics of each of these platforms, all of them are worth checking out if you plan to launch your online course. In my *Course in a Box* program, you'll find an online course platform evaluation guide to help you with selecting the perfect hosting solution for your business needs. Learn more here:

Pros and Cons of Using an Online Course Platform

There are many benefits to using a course platform. Using their system, you can simply upload your course content, including videos, workbooks, cheat-sheets, and any supplemental material you've created for your online course. They also have built-in payment processing, so once someone purchases your course, they have access immediately or on the date you designate.

Some of them offer affiliate marketing capabilities, which makes it super-easy to run an affiliate program to sell your online course. There are also options in the market to host your entire website presence, including your blog, sales funnel landing pages, and email marketing.

The primary disadvantage of using an online course platform is that you need to market your courses. That means you need to have a website or simple landing page with your lead magnet and an email service provider to collect names and email addresses. You will also be responsible for your own marketing, including building your email list and audience.

Self-Hosting with a Plug-In

You can also host your course on

your own website with a plug-in, such as Course Cats. For a self-hosting platform, you will need other integration tools, such as a place to host your videos and course files. If you're technically oriented and don't mind the upkeep of hosting your own content, this may be a good and inexpensive option for your business.

The Bottom Line

Use a marketplace platform if you simply want to teach and are not interested in building a business around your brand and name. This option also works if you want to teach and share your knowledge with the world but keep your full-time day job.

If you're technically oriented and don't mind the day-to-day management of hosting your own content, go for the DIY solution. For most business owners, I recommend utilizing an online course platform so you can focus on building your business and serving your students.

Once you have selected where you plan to host your online course and have finalized the recording of your videos, upload your course content (videos and supplemental materials) to your preferred hosting provider.

Step 5: Determine the Perfect Course Name

Now, it's time to name your course. You want to give your course a name that sells but know that your sales funnel will be the key driver of selling your online course. If you're stuck, consider these easy naming conventions:

- (your content) Lab/School/University/Academy/Institute
- (the result you are promising) in X days
- (the content) for (your target market)
- (your steps) formula/system/blueprint for (the result)
- Rock it With X
- How to create X that gets X
- Beginners/Advanced Guide to X
- DIY X
- The Ultimate Guide to X

Let's assume that your course teaches people the basics of setting up their website with Squarespace. Based on the examples above, here are some possible names for your course:

- Squarespace Lab
- Create a Squarespace Website (in a weekend)
- Squarespace Website for Wedding Photographers
- 5 Short Steps to Create Your Beautiful Squarespace Website
- Rock it With Squarespace
- DIY Squarespace
- How to Create a Squarespace Website that Converts Browsers into Clients
- Beginner's Guide to Squarespace
- The Ultimate Guide to Squarespace

Step 6: Price Your Mini-Course

Pricing your online course can be one of the hardest decisions to make. The general price points for mini-courses (aka tiny offers or starter courses) range from $27 - $47 for the B2B market (when you're marketing to businesses) and around $7 - $27 for the B2C market (when you're targeting consumers). You can still price a mini-courses at $97 and it can sell like hotcakes!

Consider the following:

- Did you intend on using it more as a lead magnet to gain instant customers?
- Did you plan to use it as a tripwire or sell it directly from a Facebook ad?

If so, it needs to be priced accordingly.

Course Creators

Story of an Online Course Creator's Journey

Anna Gray

Anna has built a successful online business using Facebook groups as her sole strategy for the past 10 years. She is the creator of "Done for you Group Content Creation," "Membership Conversation Starter," and the course "Mastering the Arts of Facebook Groups."

Follow Anna Gray of *Facebook Group Success with Anna* or on her Instagram account @ anna_b_gray

Anna is a Facebook group strategist, a 20-year operating room nurse, adoptive mother of two beautiful girls, now 17 and 14, and lives just north of Los Angeles. She describes herself as always on the go, having a hard time sitting still, a tomboy jock nerd, and always up for a challenge. In her spare time, she likes to play hockey.

Her entrepreneurial journey began when her kids were little. She had been a full-time registered nurse for 10 years, climbing the nursing ladder, changing positions every three to five years. The nursing life had taken its toll. She hit a slump and wasn't being challenged anymore in her nursing career. Unfulfilled and wanting to take a break, she was looking for something new to do. She knew nothing about network marketing or, for that matter, business but found the lifestyle of online entrepreneurs attractive. She wanted a challenge, the accolades, and most importantly, she wanted the freedom she felt it would provide her.

Being the kind of person who always strives to reach the next level, she began her next challenge. At the time, she was working as a nurse clinical systems analyst, a key role in identifying systems needs for healthcare operations. While she began her nursing career as an operating room nurse, for the last five years, she sat in the basement of a big local hospital, literally letting herself go.

She turned on to P90X and was hooked. Excited about her newfound passion, she gathered her friends and encouraged them to join her. She enjoyed the physical challenge and wanted to share this with friends and anyone else she could. She got amazing results, felt great, and knew she was living a healthy lifestyle, inspired by her newfound passion. Realizing this was an actual business, she became a Beach Body Coach, giving herself a second job. Overjoyed by the transformative results she saw in herself, it was easy to sell and get people to want to participate in Anna's coaching. All they needed to do was look at the results she achieved by following the program. She also knew that coaching would keep her accountable in maintaining her healthy results.

So, she dove into the business side and started to reach out and listen to people's success stories. When she looks back at this experience, this is how she describes the connection she created with people: "I built my business solely on Facebook groups and, you know, they were accountability groups." She was on to something with her "accountability groups." She would invite people into her group and motivate them to do challenges before challenges were even popular. Mastering the art of motivating people, she became especially good at gathering groups of people. The added bonus, she was also showing her daughters what a good role model was while promoting health and fitness and inspiring the community. Her business as a Beach Body Coach grew, she was making money, and after 4 years, she reached all the goals she had set for herself.

She reached the top 1% of the company, the goal she set for herself. It took her 4 years to get there, but she was there, even hitting a financial goal of matching her nurse management salary. Meeting her goals, it was time for the next challenge. She was still working as a nurse, working out every day on social media as a coach, but the grind was getting to her. Her kids were in elementary school, and she was making great money as a coach, so she decided to quit her nursing job. She made the decision to do coaching full-time. So, in August of 2015, she quit her job and stayed home with her kids. For the next 3 years, she worked as a full-time Beach Body Coach, making six figures. She was able to be home with her kids as they transitioned from elementary school to junior high, which was very important to her.

Five years later, after her kids had settled into junior high, she was burned out from coaching. Working out in front of the camera every day, for so many years, had gotten old. She missed nursing and decided to go back, but this time back to where she started—the operating room. She was still making really good money in her network marketing business, but she was missing the operating room. She was a staff nurse with no management, no responsibilities, just working at a hospital that she had never worked at before, with no extra responsibilities.

Life happens, and most people can understand what this means. Anna was struggling with some life issues and became completely burned out while working out. She loved being a nurse, but she needed something more. She felt the push to do something outside of nursing. While nursing was a stressful career, she wasn't looking to change it. She simply needed to do something that was fulfilling outside of nursing. She wanted to give herself something that she could be proud of and stretch herself, so she decided to build her own business. Unsure of what that business was, she knew she had lots of experience and knowledge from her network marketing. It had to be something she could do while still working as a full-time nurse and be there for her kids.

Having a gift for gathering people together, building communities, and coaching, she put her energy into teaching Facebook groups. Now she had to figure out who she was going to teach. Never shying away from a challenge, she decided to build her audience from scratch, wanting to teach the importance of Facebook groups to business owners. Narrowing down her ideal group member and who her ideal audiences were, her business was starting to unfold. She still had a lot to learn, but she now had the direction she wanted to take; she was going to become a Facebook Group Guru. The person everyone wants to seek out to help them establish their Facebook group communities.

Anna wanted to encourage her audience to be themselves and create the life they've envisioned, even if they had a busy lifestyle. If they set goals and managed their time, they too could have it all. She was setting herself as an example by working full-time in a trauma center while building a brand, a new business, new groups, and a new audience. Her clients get to see first-hand that if she can accomplish this, so can they.

Unsure of what she was going to sell, she connected with her Facebook group communities, and listened to her audience, listened to their needs, and paid attention to their pain points. This is when she realized that she could sell how to build a Facebook group and monetize her business. Most importantly, she could share the importance of human connection and the value of a community, through this social media platform, in an online space. Online connection- and relationship-building was her specialty. Being authentic, sharing her journey, and inspiring others to follow theirs, she had finally found her mission.

Having a clear vision of her audience and following her gut, Anna stopped over-thinking, asked questions, and more importantly, listened to the needs and wants of her audience. Interacting in a real environment, wanting to help people, and being herself were the secrets to her success. She still went through periods of trial and error, but she learned to push ahead, adapt, and embrace challenges head-on . A common theme within her Facebook group community is failure, which is human nature. Anna encourages her audience to look at failures as learning opportunities.

2020 had been all about visibility for her. Wanting to be known as the Facebook Group Go-To-Person, she studied how to become visible, and she took steps to make it happen. By the end of 2020, she had crossed that bridge and established the visibility she was seeking.

In 2021 she looks forward to tweaking her business by making sure she has good content and great courses. Her goal is to continue to gain visibility and focus on her one-on-one strategy. She's excited to see the transformation and progress of her students, especially those she has worked with over the past year. She looks forward to continuing to coach and connect with people and different communities.

When she started teaching Facebook groups, she took a leap of faith and made a conscious decision that she wasn't going to walk away and quit. When her first course launched and she had a difficult time selling it, instead of falling apart, she re-evaluated her business and looked at what her audience needed. Then, she pushed on, building her business, successfully launching her online courses, coaching, and continuing to inspire others.

Her biggest advice for other online course creators or online entrepreneurs is to "stop overthinking things and start doing things… without the fear of failure." As the famous hockey player Wayne Gretzky said:

"You miss every shot you don't take."

Key Takeaway and Action Items

This chapter focused on creating your initial product for your online course business. The goal is to keep moving forward and not get stuck on any tech issues or "How do I do this?" If you're not great at creating your online course lesson slides, go to Fiverr or Upwork and outsource this task. Don't get stuck in analysis paralysis when it comes to selecting an online course platform. It's not important, and it will not affect the success of your online course business. Specific action items for creating your online course include:

1. Create your online course outline

2. Create your online course teaching content

3. Record your lesson videos

4. Select your hosting option & upload course content

5. Determine the perfect course name

6. Price your mini-course

Chapter 7: Getting Your Online Course Ready to Sell

So far, you've created your online course and set it up on your preferred hosting platform, or perhaps you're self-hosting on your own website. In this chapter, I will walk you through how to get your mini-course ready to sell so you can find students and start generating revenue for your business. I will keep this simple; we will not set up a complicated sales funnel. This step will help you set up your basic online course sales funnel (essentially a soft launch) that you can build upon as you get further along in your online course journey.

Another benefit of setting up this basic funnel for your email list and social media followers is that it gives you an opportunity to test your offer with your organic (aka non-paid) traffic. Before you start with Facebook or Instagram ads, it's important to test organically and confirm that there are people who want what you're selling. I call this a soft launch; it's when you set up a simple sales funnel and launch to your warm traffic to validate that there are people who are willing to pay for what you have to offer. Let's begin by scheduling your soft-launch date.

Schedule Your Online Course Launch Date

Before you begin your online course launch plan, you need to put a stake in the ground and schedule your launch date. This is the date that your online course will be available to sell. Next, you will decide on your cart close date. It's important to have a cart open and close date as this will create urgency for your offer and force a decision.

The cart open and close time frame can last anywhere from 7-14 days. Your action item is to write down your course launch dates, including your cart open and close dates in your calendar. These dates will drive the timing of your social-media posts and launch emails.

Before we jump into all the tools and marketing material needed to set up your online course sales funnel, let's talk about the buyer's journey and why understanding this journey is important.

The Buyer's Journey

If you asked, "What in the world is the buyer's journey?", you're not alone. This is a foreign concept to many course creators. The buyer's journey is a step-by-step process that people go through when making a purchase decision.

1. First, they become aware that they have an issue and define their problem.
2. Next, in the consideration stage, they will start researching options to solve their migraine.
3. In the final step, the decision stage, they will choose a solution.

AWARENESS STAGE

Prospect becomes aware that they have an issue and are experiencing pain. They start conducting research to understand their problem.

CONSIDERATION STAGE

In this stage, they are aware they have an issue; they're researching all available options to solve their defined migraine.

DECISION STAGE

In this stage, they've decided on how they are going to solve their migraine; they are researching all possible brands/vendors who can solve this issue and will make a purchase decision.

To help you understand this, think about the steps you go through to buy a new car.

AWARENESS STAGE:

First, you realize that your car has 180,000 miles on it and it's falling apart (true story...I just got rid of my car that had 180,000 miles!).

CONSIDERATION STAGE:

In the consideration stage, you research several alternatives. For instance, do you want a car, truck or SUV? You may put together a list of must haves or nice to haves.

 OR

DECISION STAGE:

In the decision stage, once you've decided on the brand of car you want, you search for that specific car maybe even going to multiple car dealerships until you find EXACTLY what you're looking for.

To understand the buyer's journey for your online course, I want you to put yourself in the mind of your ideal customer and answer the questions below.

Awareness Stage

In the awareness stage, here are the questions you should answer for your online course:

- How does your ideal customer describe their problem/migraine?
- How does your ideal customer conduct research related to these problems?
- What are the consequences if they don't act or do anything about their problem/migraine?
- Are there any common misconceptions they have about addressing this challenge?
- How does your target customer decide whether the problem/migraine should be prioritized?

Consideration Stage

Next, move on to the consideration stage and answer these questions:

- What options does your ideal customer consider to fix their problem/migraine?
- How does your ideal customer educate themselves on these various options?
- How does your ideal customer perceive the pros and cons of each option?
- How does your ideal customer decide which option is right for them?

Decision Stage

Finally, in the decision stage, the answers to these questions will help:

- What criteria does your ideal customer use to evaluate the available offers? (e.g., ease of solution, price, etc.)

- When ideal customers investigate your offer, what do they like about it compared to other alternatives? What concerns do they have with your offer?
- Who needs to be involved in the decision? For each person involved, how does their perspective on the decision differ?
- Does your target customer have expectations around service guarantees?
- Outside of purchasing, does your student need to make additional preparations prior to purchasing your solution?

It's important to know that your social media followers or website visitors may not be ready to buy your course as soon as they meet you. You need time to walk them through the buyer's journey above. You will do this in your online course sales funnel through your marketing material—emails, social media posts, and your online course sales page.

Here are the tools and marketing material you will need for your basic sales funnel so you can convert potential prospects into paying students:

1. Marketing material: marketing copy for your sales page, emails, and social media posts. You'll also need images and possibly videos for social media and your sales page.
2. Landing-page builder for your sales page. Many online course platforms have landing-page builders that you can use for your sales page. Other possibilities include a landing-page builder like Leadpages.
3. An email service provider that can handle tags, automations, and sequences.
4. A way to accept payments. If you're using an online course platform, this feature is most likely part of their platform.

The following diagram outlines the basic email online course sales funnel so you can sell (and validate) your mini-course:

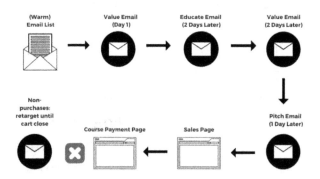

Create Your Online Course Sales Page

You may be asking, "What's a sales page?" This is a one-page site that describes your course to your ideal customer. It has one goal—convert the visitor into a paying customer (if they are the right fit for your course). If your sales page is poorly written or designed and does not speak to the pain points of your ideal customer, you will lose the prospect and miss out on the course sale.

Key Elements of a High-Converting Sales Page

I will walk you through some of the key elements of a high-converting sales page.

1. **Countdown Clock:** Include your countdown clock in the header of your sales page to create urgency and let them know when the cart is closing. For instance, you will open your cart, which means that your online course is available for purchase on x date, and you will close the cart on x date. Typically, the timeframe for cart open and close is around one week, but it can run up to 14 days. This is important because it has been proven that if people are not given a deadline to decide, they will procrastinate and never pull the trigger!

06	16	45	45	ENROLL NOW!
DAYS	HOURS	MINUTES	SECONDS	

2. **An Attention-Grabbing Headline:** After your countdown clock, at the top of your sales page, include your perfect attention-grabbing headline and hook.

3. **Talk to Their Pain Points:** Be sure in your copy that you are speaking to your ideal customer's pain points, fears, frustrations, and desires. For instance, let's say that you are selling a course on how to monetize your blog. Your focus on the sales page will talk about how their life is today (no money even though they are working hard to create their blog posts) and how it can transform after they start making money from their blog.

Where will you get the inspiration for the copy on your sales page? By talking to your ideal customer! In this example, it is bloggers who want to monetize their blogs! Ask them about their pain points and how they will feel after their blog starts creating the kind of income they deserve.

4. **Instructor's Bio and Qualifications:** Your students want to relate to you and know

that you are qualified to teach them the information. If you have any press or accolades, use them here to establish your credibility.

5. **Showcase Your Testimonials:** Social proof is key in giving your online course credibility. When you can show that your students achieve the results you promise, others are more likely to buy. 90% of consumers admit online customer reviews influence their buying decisions. If you don't have any testimonials, ask a few members of your audience if they would be interested in reviewing your course and providing a testimonial.

6. **Describe Your Course Content:** In this section, you will talk about the modules and what's included so that your students understand what they will learn and accomplish. Videos are also great to showcase what's included in your course content.

After your course content, you can place additional testimonials (if you have them) or start showcasing your bonus material. Examples of bonus material may include a private Facebook group for your paid customers, templates, or additional how-to training material.

7. **Your Call-to-Action (CTA):** In this section, you will link to your payment plans. Have a clear CTA that is worded in the first person, for example, "I'm ready to enroll now!" Research has shown that wording your CTA button in the first-person increases click-through rates by 90%.

Also, include the countdown clock again outlining when the cart will close for your online course. You can include bonuses and incentives that close on x date to encourage early sales of the course. This also creates scarcity (your course won't be available to them forever) and generates the FOMO (fear of missing out).

For most courses, it is recommended that you provide two payment options. 1) paid-in-full option usually at a discount, and 2) the payment plan option, which is a little higher than the paid-in-full option. An example may be a paid-in-full price of $997 or a payment plan of $197 for six months. One caveat to this is when you're offering a low-cost mini-course. In this case, you would simply list the price of your offers, such as $47 or $37.

8. **Highlight Your Satisfaction Guarantee:** This demonstrates your commitment to their success and how much you believe they will achieve the results you promise.
9. **Include a Chat Bot for Questions:** Be sure you have a way for customers to contact you if they have questions. Buying decisions are often emotional.

Chat software allows you to instantly communicate with the customer when they are ready to click the "enroll now" button. If this is not an option for you, you can add a frequently asked questions section.

10. **Use High-Quality Images:** Throughout your sales page, use high-quality images. Even with a digital product like an online course, customers like to see what they are buying. It's important to provide a mock-up of your online course displaying the branding.

In addition to your sales page, you also need marketing copy for your emails and social media posts. Let's cover this below.

Prepare Your Sales Emails and Social Media Posts

For your social media post captions and your sales emails, you will use the questions listed above from the buyer's journey to guide your marketing copy. For instance, for your value and educate emails in the online course sales funnel, you will focus on the questions listed in the awareness and the consideration stages of the buyer's journey. In your pitch email and the emails sent before cart closing, you will focus on the decision-stage questions, such as answering objections, service guarantees, and evaluating alternatives.

Setting Up the Sales Funnel

So far, you've created your marketing content for your sales page, your social media posts, and your emails. Now it's time to set everything up and get your course ready to sell.

First, you'll need to create your sales page. You can create your sales page on a landing-page builder like Leadpages or use your online course platform. If you're not technically inclined, you can hire someone on Fiverr or Upwork to help you with this. Make sure that you tie your sales page into your online course platform cart, so it's ready to purchase.

Next, you'll schedule your emails in your email service provider. Let's assume that your cart opens on a Wednesday and closes the following Wednesday. You would start your value and educate emails the week before the cart opens. Your first pitch email would be on the cart-open date, and you would continue to promote your course through email and social media until the cart-close date, which is approximately one week after your cart opens. Lastly, you will schedule your social media posts. You can use a social media scheduler, and there are tons of them in the marketplace.

Course Creators

The Story of an Online Course Creator's Journey
James Pollard

James Pollard is the founder of

https://theadvisorcoach.com, a marketing consultancy

that works specifically with financial advisors to help

them get more clients. He's also the host of The

Financial Advisor Marketing Podcast, which has more

than 100 episodes. Since January of 2021, his company has served over 31,000 financial advisors across the world, providing them with a suite of products to help them succeed.

Interested in marketing at an early age, James Pollard studied many of the old-school marketers who shaped his career and ignited his passion for marketing. When he was a teenager, he got started with Google AdSense and started building websites, learning how online platforms worked, and marketing them to earn some extra money. He loved it, but more importantly, he loved the money that came with it, and he was very successful at it. He graduated college in three years, receiving a major in psychology with a minor in advertising.

Prior to starting his own business, he worked in the marketing department at a major casino. His experience working in this environment, seeing all walks of life, people betting $100,000 on a hand of blackjack, gambling their rent, and trying to satisfy their addiction, led him to want to help people. He was interested to see what made people tick and learned he was good at connecting with people and passionate about the financial services market. This is when he began to learn more about financial advisors, researching the career, and studying the pain points within the industry.

He started working with a financial advisor who needed help marketing his business. In 2015, he began one-on-one coaching with financial advisors, teaching them how their website should be, what their scripts should say, how to set up their landing page, and how to overcome many of the marketing challenges they would most likely face. While the one-on-one coaching went well, he was struggling with scaling his business and knew he could reach and serve more people with an online course.

Being passionate about the financial services sector and an astute student, he noticed a disconnect between the marketing training given to new financial advisors, specifically affecting the retention rate. What he discovered is anywhere from 80 to 90% of financial advisors quit, drop out, or fail, within the first three years. He came to the conclusion that the training, marketing materials, as well as the advice the advisors were given from agencies were outdated. This, he believed to be the main problem with the retention rate, giving him the opportunity to create the business "The Advisor Coach." Starting out as a one-on-one coaching service, it would develop into an information products business, focused solely on financial advisors.

Creating products to help financial advisors market their business, "The Ultimate Financial Advisors Guide to Getting More Clients" would become the first of many products. He would turn his coaching package into an e-book and begin selling that as one of his product offerings. He had found his niche market, and after adding some 1,000 people to his email list, he began to send out surveys with questions like: Do you want to learn more about productivity? Would you like to learn how to get clients with LinkedIn? An overwhelming amount of people were interested in learning how to get clients with LinkedIn. So, he continued creating more courses, building his suite of products.

The buyers' journey evolved over time, with different sales funnels that operate differently. On the main website, the products page is set up with a survey, asking people to answer a few questions about themselves and their business. Depending on their answers, they are then directed to the product that best fits their needs—his main goal: to create products that help people and solve their problems. He also sends emails every day to people who opt in to his email list, with something tangible, something valuable. Whether it's a story, or information, or a link to a product, he stays in touch with them, building relationships, all done through evergreen sales funnels. He has different sales that happen at different points in the year. He also offers a newsletter to his financial-advisor audience. One of the perks of his newsletter is people are given the ability to ask questions and email him.

He has spent the last few years optimizing his evergreen sales funnels in order to have a system set up that is automated, with a good email sequence in place to generate traffic. His success did not happen overnight but evolved over time, creating his first course and then adding to it, one step at a time. The majority of his audience connects with his company through LinkedIn. He has used various tracking software over the years like Wicked Report, Improve Lee, and others to determine the most significant traffic source and whether the reach was through organic or paid advertising. The webinar funnel of paid ads often translates only to a handful of purchases. However, he continues with retargeting articles, through emails, some click on paid ads and knows that even if a large percentage does not buy, a percentage of people will come back. Often they see him on LinkedIn because a colleague shared a post he had made. He is constantly tweaking his touch points for people to take action.

Today with over 100+ blog articles and 100+ podcast episodes, and tens of thousands of website visitors per month, he has mastered his business. His secret? He is constantly reviewing his business statistics, evaluating conversion rates, advertising dollars, email list counts, and is always looking at the data, how the metrics affect the percentage of click-throughs, emails, inbound marketing, testing, and sales. People must know and understand the metrics of their business and how to monitor and test them continuously. He stresses the focus on productivity below:

"Don't let your emotion dictate which input you put into your business. Focus on productivity that gives you the most results for your business… let the data drive what you should be doing."

Key Takeaway and Action Items

This chapter focused on getting your mini-course ready to sell so you can find students and start generating revenue for your business. We set up a simple, non-complicated sales funnel with a sales page and an email sequence.

Specific action items for creating your simple online-course sales funnel include:

7. Schedule your cart open and close dates

8. Create your sales page for your online course

9. Prepare your sales emails and social media posts

10. Schedule your sales emails and social media posts

Chapter 8: How to Find Your Perfect Students

In this chapter, I will walk you through how to find your perfect students for your mini-course. In the previous chapter, you worked on your simple sales funnel and validated your course concept by selling it organically. Now you know that people want what you're selling! Even if you had just a few sales, I want you to take this opportunity to interact with your students and ask for testimonials. You can add your testimonials to your sales page for social proof.

Your audience is likely quite small at this point in your online course business journey, and that's ok. In this chapter, I'll walk you through how to sell your mini-course without having a large email list or social media following.

There are two main ways to sell your mini-course when your email list and social media following are small or basically non-existent.

1. Affiliate marketing
2. Facebook and Instagram ads

Let's first start with affiliate marketing.

Affiliate Marketing

One of the best ways to sell your online course when you're just starting out is using other people's audiences. This is called affiliate marketing.

Affiliate marketing can be a win-win for both parties. You give your affiliate an opportunity to make easy money, and you're able to find the perfect students for your online course without huge ad spends or other marketing costs.

Why Use Affiliates to Sell Your Online Course

The greatest advantage of using an affiliate program to sell your online course is that you don't need to have a giant-size pre-launch email list or use paid advertising to find the perfect students to start selling your online course.

Your affiliates can earn a truly passive income because they don't have to be involved in supporting the students; they can simply sell your online course and hand off any student support functions to you.

This performance-based marketing approach provides a strong incentive for them to promote your course, and you only have to pay for what they earned.

Affiliate marketing broadens your reach, and you can reach audiences that you would have had to pay thousands of dollars in marketing costs to find otherwise.

Another huge benefit is that affiliate marketing provides a reputation boost; affiliates help spread the word about you and your products or services. This helps build trust and confidence in your online course.

Affiliate marketing is extremely cost-effective. You save money by not having to spend it on ads to market your products; you only pay out of pocket (i.e., commission) when your online course is sold.

One last benefit of affiliate marketing is the increased traffic to your website, which is tracked by your Facebook pixel. This allows you to retarget anyone who visited your website but didn't purchase at a later date.

How to Find the Best Affiliates

Finding the right people to promote your products or services is a little tricky. Why? All affiliates are not the same. Some people may sign up for your affiliate program because you provide a sizeable commission but may not have the perfect audience for your course. Here are a few places to look for the right affiliates:

- Social media platforms – join Facebook or LinkedIn groups within your market, connect with influencers, and follow businesses within your industry and other professionals.
- Create a LinkedIn account – this platform is more business-

focused than other social media platforms and is a great place to network with others in your niche.

- Connect with bloggers and podcasters who have a similar audience to your perfect student – they tend to have larger audiences, which gives you a sizeable pool of potential students.
- Affiliate forums – go to places where affiliates hang out. That is an easy way to connect with affiliates, especially since they use these forums to discuss marketing tactics from more experienced affiliate marketers.
- Competitors – look at what your competition is doing. See what types of incentives they employ to get affiliates to market their products and see how you can add more to entice them to promote your products.
- Online affiliate summits – a great place to connect with affiliates if your products and services align with what they are seeking.

I have found that, hands down, the best way to find the perfect affiliates is to reach out to other influencers, bloggers, podcasters, or businesses in your niche and ask them if they would be interested in participating in your affiliate launch. I've connected with them by following them on social media and joining their email list. It was important that I got to know them first to see if they would truly be a good fit for what I was promoting.

When you reach out to prospective affiliates, be sure to focus on what's in it for them and why you think their audience would be interested in the course you're selling. Highlight the fact that all marketing material would be provided for them, and the only thing they would be responsible for doing is promoting on social media and to their email list.

Ways to Reward Your Affiliates and How Much to Pay

To attract affiliates and promotion of your online course, attractive compensation is key. Here are some tips in deciding how much to offer your affiliates:

- You can create different levels of pay for your affiliates. Make sure you factor in your profit margin when deciding to pay commissions based on productivity. This type of commission lets your affiliate marketers know that their extra efforts in promoting your online course will result in a higher payout. For example, if your affiliate sold 100 courses, the commission would be 40%. If they sold over 100 courses, the commission would be 50%.
- Research your competitors and see how much they pay their affiliate marketers. Having this information can help you gauge how much to charge, but make sure it is in alignment with your financial interests. As a

benchmark, most affiliate programs for online courses are between 40-50%.

- Provide your affiliates with gifts from your brand for achieving certain milestones. Examples include t-shirts, coffee mugs, water bottles, pens, keychains, etc.
- Create bonuses for your top affiliates as an extra incentive for them to market and sell your online course. Going beyond the typical commission is a great way to reward your affiliates who make an effort.
- Provide recognition, such as a leader board showcasing the top affiliate performers.
- Gamify your incentives. There is nothing like a little competition between your affiliates. Provide them with a certain type of badge for reaching a particular level in affiliate marketing. Provide leaderboards and titles. These are great ways to engage your affiliates.

How to Set Up Your Affiliate Marketing Program

In order to pay your affiliates and track which online course sales come from them, you need an affiliate tracking system. Let's walk through the steps to set up your affiliate marketing program.

Step 1. Choose your affiliate platform (e.g., ThriveCart, SendOwl, or ShareASale, or even your online course platform)

Take a look at what your competitors are using and determine what is best for your business. When you use an affiliate marketplace, they are easy to set up, and there is no need to track your sales. The affiliate payments are processed for you.

When selecting your online course platform, it's important to note that many of them offer affiliate tools and management if you plan to launch with affiliates. If your online course platform offers this option, I highly recommend going this route.

Here's how affiliate tracking works

for many affiliate platforms:

- You have them create a share link on your platform to share with their audiences.
- This link will place a cookie with the prospects' browser for a certain number of days.
- If their customer purchases from your site using the same browser, and the purchase is made within that period, the transaction is counted as an affiliate transaction, and they earn a commission.

Step 2. Determine how you will pay your affiliates

You have several options for your affiliate compensation, such as one-time, recurring (subscription-based), or once they reach a certain amount.

Step 3. Decide on your affiliate program guidelines

Do not skip this step! I recommend finding a trusted source to create your affiliate program contract. Each affiliate will need to sign your contract before enrolling in your affiliate program. My go-to resource for legal templates for online course creators is Artful Contracts, and you can learn more about my suggested legal tools here.

Step 4. Craft your marketing material

To support your affiliates, all the marketing material should be created and personalized for them. This includes email swipes, social media captions and images, and customized affiliate links so your affiliate system can track and credit sales.

Consider putting together an affiliate welcome package along with a private Facebook or Slack group for your affiliates, where they can ask questions and get support during your promotional period.

Affiliate marketing can be a powerful tool to find the perfect students for your online course, especially when you're just starting out and your audience is small or nonexistent.

Keep in mind that you still need a sales page and other materials to promote your online course with affiliate marketing. We will cover what is needed to sell your online course later in the book.

Now, let's talk about another strategy to sell your online course when you're just starting out.

Facebook and Instagram Ads

Hands down, Facebook and Instagram ads are one of the best ways to find the perfect students for your online course. Many new entrepreneurs shy away from ads in the beginning because of the investment. But what if you were able to add new subscribers to your email list every day with little to no money out of your pocket? The solution: creating a sales funnel that pays for itself.

The best way for me to explain this is to show you two examples directly from my own business. There are two ways to do this.

1. You can set up a tripwire
2. You can sell your mini-course directly from an ad

Let's first walk through a tripwire example:

Your target audience sees your Facebook or Instagram ad and clicks on your call to action.

You take them to the landing page for your free offer.

NEED A PLUG-N-PLAY SYSTEM FOR CREATING YOUR ONLINE COURSE IN AS LITTLE AS A WEEK?

How relieved would you feel knowing you had simple step-by-step system to create your online course and help you select your perfect online course platform without wasting hours and hours of your time?

One that helps you create a revenue generating online course to make your 2019 goals attainable and brings in revenue to your business?

Limited Time Offer (FREE) Normally $99.

YES! I NEED THIS!

LET ME GUESS...

- You've had "create an online course" on your to do list for some time, but haven't started.

- You're stuck on (fill in the blank) -- selecting an online course platform, creating your slides, recording your videos, preparing your course outline or maybe you're even still trying to figure out your profitable

They sign up for the free offer, and on the next page (which is often referred to as a Thank-You page), they see this:

WAIT! BEFORE YOU GO, HERE'S A SPECIAL OFFER JUST FOR YOU. (P.S.
Check your email for your Course in a Box login)

HOW MUCH TIME WOULD YOU SAVE WITH PLUG AND PLAY TEMPLATES AND SWIPE FILES FOR YOUR ONLINE COURSE SALES FUNNEL?

40 hours or more? The first time I created an online course sales funnel, the webinar presentation alone took me 20 hours to complete!

This didn't even count the countless sales funnel emails I

needed to write, a month's worth of social media posts, or

the days I spent creating the long form sales page.

By the time I got to my first webinar presentation, I was exhausted and burnt out. And I still needed to get through another live webinar presentation and had another week before my cart closed!

I thought..."There HAS to be a better way!"

And now there is...

Hurry! This special offer is available until 08/7/2019   **00 22 41 22**

On the tripwire sales page, you have something that says. "WAIT! Before you go…" with a limited-time offer to create urgency. Once they're on your email list, you tag them with the offer they opted into and/or purchased and start your email nurture sequence. The diagram looks like this:

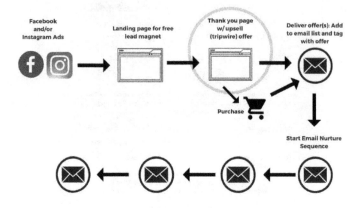

In the diagram above, your mini-course is the tripwire offer, which is an instant customer from your Facebook ad. As you get further along in your online course journey, you can add an order bump (an additional mini-course or digital products), and other upsells to increase your average order value.

2. The Mini-Course (directly from an ad) Example

Another option is to sell your mini-course directly from a Facebook and Instagram ad. They are added to your customer list, and you will nurture them through your follow-up emails, which may include coaching them through your online course material.

Here's what this looks like. Your target audience sees your ad and clicks on the "Learn More" button or the link in your ad.

They are directed to the sales page for the digital product. This is a longer-form sales page, and there's a limited-time special offer.

Once they've purchased the mini-course, you add them to your email list, tag them with the offer they purchased, and start your email nurture sequence. It looks like this:

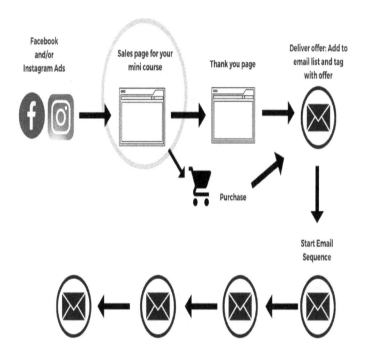

I've tested both options above in my business, and both converted very well. If your main goal is list-building, I suggest leading with a free offer (you'll get more sign-ups) and then offer the tripwire.

Tools Required to Set Up Your Facebook Ad Sales Funnel

Here are the tools required for setting up your Facebook Ad funnel.

1. Landing page provider like Leadpages.net. You can also use your own website or a landing-page builder from your online course platform like Kajabi. You will use the landing-page builder for your sales page and sign-up page for your lead magnet, in addition to your thank-you page. You should already have these set up from your simple sales funnel we created in Chapter 7.

2. Your Facebook pixel set up and your event tracking.

3. A countdown timer to create urgency in your offer.

4. A way to accept payment for your mini-course (most course platforms have this integrated with their service). This should be set up from your simple sales funnel we created in Chapter 7.

5. An email service provider where you can create sequences and assign tags. Again, already set up from Chapter 7.
6. Facebook Business Manager account to set up your Facebook and Instagram ads.
7. Ad copy and creative
8. Your mini-course!

Selling your online course through a Facebook ad funnel is more of an advanced strategy. If you're ready to dip your toes into Facebook ads yet, start with selling your online course through affiliates. This will give you additional time to test your funnel, get testimonials, and continue to build your audience.

Key Takeaway and Action Items

This chapter focused on finding students for your mini-course even if your audience is still small. Starting with affiliate marketing is a great way to get started when your budget is tiny. This gives you an opportunity to find your ideal students, generate revenue, and continue growing your online course business.

Specific action items for setting up your affiliate program include:

11. Choose your affiliate platform

12. Determine how you will pay your affiliates

13. Decide upon your affiliate program guidelines

14. Craft your affiliate marketing material

If you decide to test selling your online course through Facebook ads, either through a tripwire or directly from an ad, consider hiring a trusted Facebook ad consultant who can help you set up and optimize your paid ads.

Chapter 9: Growing Your Online Course Business

Here's what you've accomplished so far. You've created your mini-course and your simple sales funnel. This allowed you to test and validate your offer and messaging. Then, you continued to find students either through affiliate marketing and/or paid advertising. You've learned a ton along the way! This process has allowed you to make tweaks and minor adjustments in your marketing. You also have testimonials from students who loved your mini-course and want more of what you offer.

Think about your next step. Could you set up a group coaching program bundled in with a course? Create a subject-matter course that takes your student's learning to the next level? How about a membership? The best way to figure out how to best serve your audience is to ask them. Using a survey like SurveyMonkey or Google forms, survey your audience. You could also conduct short Zoom interviews, which would provide valuable information.

Here are some questions to ask your audience to help you determine your next offer:

- What are they struggling with the most right now?
- What's keeping them from moving forward?
- Where do they want to be this time next year?

- What are their biggest pain points or frustrations?
- Would or can they pay money to fix their issue?
- What frustrates them the most?
- What is their role in the purchase decision?
- What objections would they have?

After you've gathered the results of your survey or Zoom interviews, take some time to analyze the data and reflect upon their answers. Let's assume that the data indicates that your audience needs more handholding. Could this be accomplished with a membership? How about group coaching? Or could you create a subject-matter course and bundle in a Facebook or Slack group to support them?

It's also important to consider how much support you are willing to provide. Are you willing to roll up your sleeves to support them in a group coaching program that may have a course bundled in? How does a membership program feel where you're creating content every month and supporting your members in established office hours? Or are you interested in a more hands-off type of digital course business where support is provided directly on the online course platform? All these questions should be considered before deciding on your next step.

Selecting Your Next Offer

Now is the time move forward with your next offer. It's scary, but action will create clarity. If you decide to move forward with a subject-matter course (as we defined in Chapter 5), you will follow the same process to create this course as you did with your mini-course.

Let's assume that you've decided to launch with a signature online course but creating the volume of content needed for this course overwhelms you, or you know that it will take months and months to create. Consider launching with a low-cost membership and create the content over time, for example, over one year. When you're ready, you can launch with your signature course, give your members access, and voila, the signature course that you can charge $2,000 or more for is ready!

Growing Your Online Course Business

There are several ways to proceed to find students for your next offer. Let's assume that you've decided to launch a signature course but are starting with a membership so you can have revenue coming in while you create your content. You could offer this membership on the tripwire of a Facebook ad (which we covered in Chapter 8). You could offer a webinar or a 5-day challenge to build your audience and promote your next offer. Webinars, training, workshops, masterclasses, or challenges are all good options to establish your expertise and sell your next offer.

For instance, let's assume that you've decided to create a subject-matter course. You're a Squarespace expert, and you help small businesses and new business owners create their own websites. Your mini-course focuses on helping them get started on their Squarespace site by setting up a landing page and collecting email addresses. Your subject matter course will take them through setting up their entire website. Your mini-course is priced at $37, and your subject matter course will be priced at $497.

You've decided that a masterclass, which is simply a form of online training, which walks them through the 5 Must-Have Pages for Your New Website, would be perfect to promote your new subject-matter course (Caveat: I haven't done any research in this area, nor do I consider myself a website expert, so I have no idea if this is a good training topic!). Essentially, what you're doing is setting up a more advanced sales funnel than what we did in Chapter 7.

Here's how this funnel works: You will run Facebook ads to promote your masterclass and get new people to join your upcoming training. You'll also invite your email list and your followers on social media. You will have a registration page where they sign up for your masterclass and pick their time slot (generally, you will offer 2-4 time slots). Towards the end of your masterclass, you transition over to your sales pitch, outlining the benefits and what's included in your online course. The last step is directing webinar attendees to your sales page. This is your cart open date. You will then continue to retarget non-purchasers until your cart closes.

Here's what I like about webinar funnels. You can record the training and use it in a future evergreen sales funnel, which we will discuss in Chapter 10. Webinars can quickly establish you as an expert in the field and allow you to build the know, like, and trust factor during the training presentation.

5-day challenges are also powerful for promoting your new offer. Here's what a challenge looks like. During days 1-4, you are delivering your content through email and also via the Facebook group that you have set up specifically for the challenge. On Day 5, you will deliver your content and your sales pitch for your online course. You will direct your challenge participants to your sales page. This is your cart open date. For any participants that did not purchase on Day 5, you will continue to retarget them until your sales cart closes.

For your webinar or 5-day challenge, you'll need all the funnel pieces we discussed in Chapter 7, including a sales page for your new offer and a registration page for participants to sign up for your webinar or challenge. You'll need emails prepared to invite your email list to your event and sales emails to retarget non-purchasers after your event.

How to Get Participants in Your Webinar or Challenge

To fill up your webinar or challenge, you will invite your email list and social media followers. You could also reach out to any affiliates to see if they would be willing to promote; in this case, you'd need to be willing to compensate them for their efforts by either a one-time fee or a percentage of your course sales. Hands down, the best way to fill up your webinar or challenge is through Facebook and Instagram ads. To do this, you'll need to create an ad campaign that targets your perfect students. Here are some tips to help you get started:

- Your ad campaign should be a conversion campaign (which directs Facebook to find people who're likely to sign up for your event).
- You will target cold audiences, which are people who don't know you. You can find these cold audiences by target pages they like and follow on Facebook. Note: if your Facebook pixel is seasoned (aka has traffic), you can also set up a campaign targeting your warm audience.
- Test different creative headlines and the ad copy for your ad.

- Be sure that your lead event is set up on the thank-you page so you can track conversions.

Course Creator

Story of an Online Course Creator's Journey

Ben Taylor

Founder of thehomeworkingclub.com, a global portal providing advice to remote workers and freelancers. Ben is sought after for his freelance expertise. He has published over 300 articles, hosts a podcast, and has helped and inspired over 1 million people. His freelancing course "Freelancing Kickstarter" was released in September 2020 and has over 100 students signed up.

Ben had established his career and was the owner of a very lucrative freelance business, but by 2009, he was burned out. He and his wife decided to move to Portugal. While his wife had managed to persuade her company to allow her to work remotely, he was faced with staring at his laptop, searching for ways to make money online. Creating a blog called "Moving to Portugal" for family and friends, he gained what he calls accidental momentum. People were interested in his blog, and he ended up receiving a lot of traffic from it.

His next blog, he decided, would be more calculating as he really wanted to create something that would help people. With years of freelancing experience, he created a site about freelancing and home working, targeting people who wanted to learn more about remote, online work from home. His slogan was "disrupt with integrity" as he was determined to share the truth about freelancing and not sugar-coat the subject. The content he would provide to his audience would be authentic and truthful, focusing on the pros and cons, hardships, and benefits of this type of business. His blog was created, and his website homeworkclub.com was born.

He learned how to master the art of content for SEO and link-building, and gained a social media presence. By starting a podcast, he brought a lot of traffic to his site, establishing his niche market. People were interested in learning about all the aspects of freelancing, and his blog and podcast became successful. The traffic created was often from people searching via Google, finding him through specific articles he posted.

He created his first online course, "Freelance Kickstarter," after running a couple of surveys from his readers. This course covered many elements on how to start freelancing, such as: how to set up your rates, how to identify different types of clients, how to fire clients, and so on. He also wanted to distinguish himself from other competitors and not make any promises, unlike many of the freelance courses out there. He gave his audience a step-by-step course on all the ins and outs of being a freelancer, with all the pros and cons. After about a year, he was ready to launch his course; however, it was nine months preceding Covid, and everything was changing rapidly.

The effects of the pandemic had a more profound effect on his business than he had anticipated. This was the time where he was launching his course. Working from home was a much sought-after topic with the lockdowns from the pandemic. He was established as a go-to source; however, he began to experience competition from large corporations. Forbes, The New York Times, The Washington Post, everyone was writing about working from home, or home working. He recalls feeling like he was a "mom and pop" burger restaurant surrounded by Wendy's and McDonald's. The competition was relentless. While he had an audience established through his blogging and podcasts, the main problem was the big players were now also blogging about his topic. Unfortunately, this changed his rankings on the Google landing page. He became a small fish in a much bigger pond overnight.

With his course 95% completed, he did a beta testing by sending out emails to people on his email list to see if they would be interested in his course. He was quite surprised as he expected only a handful of people, and he ended up having over 200 volunteers. Fifteen people was a good start and all he would need, making sure they would get back to him and test the course in the time frame that he needed. It was important to him to make sure that people were going to be happy with the course and how it was presented. He also wanted to get an idea of pricing. So, on the Google form he sent out around to the beta testers, he asked them how much they thought he should be charging for his course. Looking for a fair way to assess his course price, he utilized his beta testers to get comments that he could use on his testimonial page. He planned his email sequence to go into his email list, but the email funnels went terribly wrong. Despite him checking out his delivery sequence down to the last details, people were not getting the emails in the sequence that he had set up. Being a bit embarrassed and sending out email apologies, he set out to make things right.

He did not charge the beta testers who were road testing his course and provided them with free access. Wanting to make sure that people didn't feel short-changed by getting written lessons instead of videos, he was pleasantly surprised to learn that people preferred to have both. Now convinced he had the right medium, for the right lessons, with constructive feedback, he launched his course on Teachable with the ability to add affiliates. Besides, he also created promotional offers through his email list by setting up sales funnels for people who sign up through his website. On some of his relevant articles, he posts a call to action, which leads them to the core sales page.

He set up his price points by surveying beta testers, finding that the most popular pricing for his particular course was between $147 and $197. So, he decided that $147 would be the appropriate price to charge for his course. People visiting his website can go right to his lead magnet, and the steps are created to take them through the nurture sequence where they can buy the course. They can also go directly to an article that will also link them to the course. He runs occasional promotions, but for the most part, has created a set price. This set price was specifically created based on the feedback from people who have taken his course.

His advice to anyone starting an online course business is to simply rise above the inevitable imposter syndrome. This way of thinking will always stop you from reaching your goal. He also stresses not to undervalue the knowledge and experience that you have. You're not going to make money from an idea; you have to execute as well. Many people get stuck in the idea stage and don't take it any further. You must start.

Key Takeaway and Action Items

This chapter focused on growing your online course business and selecting your next offer. We talked about how to promote your offer through a webinar or 5-day challenge. Your action items for these next steps include:

- Surveying your audience to determine how you can best serve them

- Analyze the survey data and decide on your next offer

- Build your next offer, including marketing material, such as your sales page and sales emails

- Promoting your new offer through a webinar or challenge

- Filling up your webinar or challenge through your email list, social media following, and a webinar or 5-day challenge

To fill up your webinar or challenge using Facebook ads, consider hiring a trusted Facebook ad consultant.

Chapter 10: Sell Your Online Course on Autopilot

In the last chapter, you decided on your next offer and promoted it through a webinar or 5-day challenge. If you experienced fatigue and burnout during your live launch, you're not alone. They are a ton of work! If you're looking for ways to sell your online course without doing a live webinar or showing up in a Facebook group every single day for a 5-Day Challenge, in this chapter, we will talk about ways to sell your online course on autopilot, which is also called an evergreen sales funnel.

What's an Evergreen Sales Funnel?

An evergreen sales funnel is simply a sales funnel that runs in the background of your business on autopilot. When a visitor comes to your website or landing page for one of your lead magnets and signs up, you add them to your email list, and then they are added to your email nurture sequence, which promotes your online course.

The most successful evergreen sales funnels also have paid ads running in the background to keep their offer at the top of their prospect's mind, answer objections, and encourage purchase.

With an evergreen sales funnel in your business, you don't have to constantly do a live launch like a webinar or a 5-day challenge where you're stressed and exhausted from all the work involved.

Basically, it's just an automated system using your website or a landing page builder and your email service provider (and a few other tools that we'll talk about here!) to sell your online course.

My online course business

primarily runs an autopilot. Around once per year, I do a live launch like a virtual summit with a webinar, but for most of the other months, my sales are driven by my evergreen sales funnels.

I absolutely love evergreen sales funnels because they allow me to focus on what I do best, which is serving my students and creating content. I will walk you through the exact tools you need to create this high-converting, stress-free sales funnel in your business—so if you hate live launches, you're in the right place!

What Does an Evergreen Sales Funnel Look Like?

I'm partial to a video series or webinar for an evergreen sales funnel, but please note that you can set up an evergreen sales funnel even with a 5-day challenge. The only caveat that I have is that with any evergreen sales funnel I highly recommend using video throughout your funnel to quickly build that know, like, and trust factor.

In a live launch, your prospects

are seeing you live. You may be doing a 5-day challenge, where you're showing up in a Facebook group for five straight days. Or you may be doing a series of webinars where they see your face in the webinar and on Facebook lives during your launch.

When you're promoting your online course in an evergreen sales funnel, you still need that video component. That's why I love a video series or a webinar for evergreen sales funnels.

Here's what a 4-part video series evergreen sales funnel looks like:

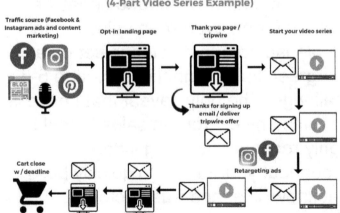

You still need a traffic source, which can be Facebook and Instagram ads, traffic from Pinterest, or you can drive traffic from your content marketing like a blog post or your podcast. I like to use all these traffic strategies to drive sign-ups to my evergreen sales funnels.

Once the visitor opts in for your video series, if you have a tripwire, offer it on the thank-you page. I'm a big fan of tripwires to help subsidize your ads, but most importantly, gain an instant customer.

Now is the time to start your video series. This is simply a series of videos that you'll send out via email during a specified time. The content in your emails and on your video landing pages should be moving your prospect toward the sale.

Toward the end of your video series, you'll introduce your offer with your sales page and continue to market your online course until the cart closes. Now, let's talk about the tools to build the perfect evergreen sales funnel (so you can sell your online course without launching).

5 Tools to Build the Perfect Evergreen Sales Funnel

Tool #1: Landing-page builder (that can host videos)

Whether you're setting an evergreen webinar funnel, an evergreen video series, or even an evergreen challenge funnel, you need a landing-page builder that can host your videos. Personally, I use Kajabi for all my landing pages, and it works great. The best part is I also use Kajabi to host my online courses, so I don't have to pay for separate software for my landing pages. Leadpages is another option for hosting your video series for your funnel.

Tool #2: Email service provider (that can handle sequences and automation)

I think it goes without saying that you need an email service provider for your evergreen sales funnel. The main thing to evaluate when considering various email service providers is to look for one that integrates with your landing page provider and can handle sequences and automation.

Tool #3: Evergreen countdown timer (so you can create urgency and FOMO with your offer)

Creating urgency is one of the most important elements of an evergreen sales funnel. Your prospect will sit on the fence and not make a decision about purchasing your online course until they are absolutely forced to.

You may have experienced this in one of your live launches. Most of your sales come at the very end and right before your cart closes. This is the same for an evergreen sales funnel.

But you may be asking, "Is the deadline a real deadline? Or am I just creating a 'fake' deadline because people can go through this funnel and buy at any time?"

The best way to handle this is to offer a price discount by the deadline or a bonus offer that your prospect only gets if they purchased by the deadline. This drives the FOMO (fear of missing out) that creates urgency and convinces your future students to purchase or else they'll miss out on your awesome course.

Tool #4: Social proof pop-up (to add real-time social proof)

Did you know that 92% of your prospects going through your online course sales funnel will read your social proof, including online reviews before making a purchase decision?

Social proof will help boost your sales because it eases the mind of your future students by letting them know that others are purchasing your online course. Your future students want proof from their peers that your online course and you are trustworthy.

Both social proof and FOMO work. But how can you display social proof? Studies have shown that customers don't necessarily trust website reviews that a firm puts on their sales page or in their emails. When someone signs up for your online course, they show "proof of purchase!"

Tool #5: Facebook pixel code (so you can retarget your website visitors)

Here's the deal. Whether you have a live launch or if you're running an evergreen sales funnel in your business, you still need traffic going through your online course sales funnel. Unless you get thousands of visitors to your website every day and get a steady stream of opt-ins, you're still going to need to run a paid ad-traffic source to sustain your online course business.

But let's say, for the sake of argument, you're getting a hundred new leads every single day. Paid ads will allow you to retarget these leads and convert them into paying customers through low-cost retargeting ads. With your Facebook pixel, you'll be able to run an ad campaign to retarget your leads and walk them through the purchase process. Make sure you have your Facebook pixel on your landing page, thank-you page, and sales page.

Course Creator

Story of an Online Course Creator's Journey

Debbie Gartner

Debbie runs a successful home décor blog. She's been blogging since 2010 and has harnessed the power of SEO to get over 500,000 page views per month and generates over $20,000 in net profit a month. She has leveraged her blog in line to pay off more than $238,000 of debt, doing this while coaching hundreds of bloggers on SEO, and is also the best-selling author of 2 very successful SEO books: "Easy on Page SEO" and "Easy Backlinks for SEO." She has sold over 3,000 e-books and courses to bloggers and entrepreneurs worldwide.

In 2011, she created a website called theflooringgirl.com. This site included a blog designed to connect with her audience and find new customers in her area, just outside of New York City. Learning to master SEO and backlinks, she gained the attention of not only a local audience but people around the country. She grew so fast she couldn't keep up with the amount of calls and questions. She hired an assistant to help her with all the traffic, especially screening inquiries; this way, she could focus just on local business, saving her time and money.

Her efforts paid off, and she became incredibly successful, but she knew she needed to take the necessary steps to keep the momentum going. She connected with reality companies, painting companies, and restoration companies and became a master marketer, utilizing her website and blog to connect with customers. However, a series of unfortunate events forced her to close down her business, leaving her $238,000 dollars in debt. So, while customers called her looking for her services, she had signed a document forcing her not to be able to compete for 2 years.

Struggling to pay her bills and devastated by her loss, she focused on her blog and website, monetizing her site, as she knew how to blog and was an expert in SEO. Her blog was still getting 150 k page views a month but wasn't monetized, so she had no revenue coming in. Researching ways she could make money with her blog, she read other blogs, took courses, and listened to hours of podcasts. She knew she had the drive, knowledge, and experience to change her circumstances. Pivoting and restructuring her business was necessary and crucial to her survival.

Through networking, she found some clients to blog for and was helping them with SEO. She also took a part-time position selling paint jobs for a local contractor. These part-time jobs managed to sustain her for 2 years while she continued to build her website blog. Monetizing her website became her primary focus. With established site traffic, she became an

Amazon Associate, bringing in $300 dollars her first month. Then she turned on the ads and increased her profit to make $1,000 dollars the next month and $1,500 dollars the month after. After turning on the ads, she was finally generating income. Her revenue stream was improving, and after 11 months, using ads and affiliate marketing to make her blogging work, she started to see her revenue stream increase to $3,100. Then it went from $4,100 to $6,600 and up to $10,000. This was all profit margin.

Still needing to make more money to pay off her debt, she happened to find a member in a Facebook group she belonged to, looking for help with SEO. In exchange for a small fee, she would help teach the ins and outs of SEO. Once word got out among the other members, she had more students seeking to learn her strategy. She added a new layer to her business, coaching people on SEO, and staying booked, three months out. This audience was encouraging her to write a blog on SEO, so she could reach out and help more people.

Not sure how her SEO coaching would fit in with her flooring blog and website, she created her first SEO e-book. She did not have an email list; instead, she launched her first book with affiliates, selling specifically through them and past customers. People would buy her book and then would go into her Facebook group and rave about how they didn't even know something like that existed.

Her first book was about backlinks, which back then people had never heard of, and no one was talking about. With backlinks, there are 2 main parts to SEO, on-page and off-page. The on-page with SEO is everything the customer experiences on a site. It's the content that's written, how well it's optimized for the keywords you want it ranked for, pictures, site speed, and everything a user experiences while on your site. The other 50% is what accounts for rankings, the off-page backlinks, which basically happens when you get a powerful backlink from another site to your site. In Google's eyes, it's like votes for your site. You want more votes and more backlinks to your site. It's not as simple as that, as not all backlinks are created equal. Basically, you want different types of links, and that is what her book was about: the importance of backlinks, how to use them, when to use them, and where to find them.

When the book launched, she initially thought it would be a failure , but to her surprise, it wasn't, and she made $14,000 the first month in profit. Seeing how powerful her e-book was, she realized that she needed to write beginner, basic SEO courses. She created an e-book on the basics for beginners and then realized it would be more successful if she bundled both books and sold them together. In February of her first year, she made $18,000 for that month and then in March, $24,000. Part of the jump was due to the new launch and the sale she ran.

She began her email list and created a free SEO course to get people interested. From there, she directed even more people to her course, with many buying her book. She created a more advanced course called "SEO Revamp," not for beginners but for people who were already getting traffic but wanted to get their articles ranked higher. This course dives deeper into all the typical questions: How do they get their articles ranked? How do they get from page two to page one? If they're on page one, how do they move up the slots? After you have three to six months of traffic, what's the next level? She answered all of these questions in her course and launched it on Teachable. The first launch of this course ended up making $6,000. Just as Debbie challenged herself with her financial goals, she applied the same challenge to her audience reach. Her mission was to service, maintain, and grow her audience, and she succeeded.

She paid off her bad debt of $238,000 in 2020 and was left only with her mortgage, which she defines as good debt. Her consistent profit for the past 22 months had been 20k a month, with a few months better than 20k. Then the pandemic hit, and things got difficult again, causing her to pivot her business once again. She saw her ad revenue go down and commissions for Amazon Associates that were once 8% went down to 3%. One of her affiliates was put on pause because they couldn't make the products. Her profits began to decrease by $12k a month. Embracing the challenge, she decided to focus more on her products, affiliates, and email lists and less on her traffic and ad revenue. Her ability to shift her business increased her profits, and she had her best month in July of 2020, earning $31k, which was in part due to an affiliate promotion she did. She had just launched her Amazon course, "Tips and Tricks from Beginner to Advanced," to create a passive income stream. She launched on Black Friday week and ended up making $45k that month.

Her answer to her success is simple: "You have to always think with a customer in mind. How am I going to help them? How am I going to teach them? What type of information am I going to share with them?" Utilizing analytics, she uses her sales funnel with her free SEO courses, and this materializes into sales. How does she get more people on her email list? How much is each subscriber worth, and how much is the ad costing her? She ended up scaling up her ads on Facebook, so while her ad spending was increasing each month, she was scaling up her email list. She was always looking for ways to improve her sales funnels, create more funnels or products, and determine what the best lead magnets were to use.

Not only did Debbie learn to diversify her business, but she also managed to scale it up in a challenging market. Knowing she wanted to keep growing, yet understanding that recessions tend to happen every four to five years, she had a plan. So, when the pandemic happened, she knew her rates would go down, and in order to be ok she knew she needed to scale up her business. While this meant she would be paying more in ads, at the same time, it also meant it would be scaling up her email list.

She credits her success to digging into the numbers and projecting the forecast for her business, as well as her continuous quest for learning and commitment to serving her audience. During this downturn, she also capitalized on her blog posts, turning them into mini e-books, selling them for $5 by offering them in a PDF format. Selling to her customer base, she was able to convince many that having this in a PDF format, stored on their computer, would be a way for them to have her e-book forever. They could use the knowledge she created as a reference at any time because it would be immediately accessible to them. She used many of these as tripwires on her Facebook ads.

Debbie has had great success selling products from $11 to $97 dollars and up. Her first offerings on her courses are often provided at a lower price point, and then she builds upon this over time as she adds more courses. She is always analyzing what products are selling and those that aren't.

Her best advice to those wanting to get started is: "Start, don't worry about making money and needing a huge product. You can sell anything."

Key Takeaway and Action Items

This chapter focused on setting up an evergreen sales funnel for your business, so you're not constantly launching. This allows you to focus on other activities in your online course business, like creating new offers and serving your students while generating revenue consistently. The good news is much of what you've already created can be repurposed for your evergreen sales funnel.

To set up your evergreen sales funnel,

you'll need:

1. Your webinar recording or a video series recording (you can repurpose content from a 5-day challenge)

2. Evergreen countdown timer

3. Social proof

4. Traffic source (e.g., Facebook and Instagram ads)

5. Facebook pixel code (including event code) installed

Here's a hot tip: consider adding your mini-course as a tripwire in your evergreen sales funnel to offset the cost of your Facebook ads!

Chapter 11: #1 Skill Needed for Success

By now, you've created your mini-course and launched it into the market. You have a solid way to attract new customers to your business. Your understanding of sales funnels and how to use them to sell your online course has expanded. You may have even dipped your toes into paid advertising to help find your perfect students for your business.

If you ever get stuck, my best suggestion is just to take action. You may not get it perfect the first time. As I've said before, action creates clarity, and you'll learn from each failed launch or know what to tweak for the next time.

Don't forget about the many ways you can get support for your business. Finding private Facebook, LinkedIn, or Slack groups can help guide you on your journey. If tech is not your strong suit, hire someone on Upwork or Fiverr to do the job. The internet is filled with a vast network of resources; take advantage of them and remember you are not alone.

Seeking knowledge and educating yourself will be a constant quest on your journey as an entrepreneur.

Just remember that you need continual traffic coming into your business. You can drive new email subscribers through SEO and content marketing, public-relations activities, and social media, both organic and paid. This is a difficult part of the process, especially in today's crowded market. It is also where many business owners tend to lose their self-confidence, become discouraged, and tend to give up.

How to Pivot Your Business

So, you've followed all the steps outlined in this book, and you've launched your online course business. You've managed to get it up and running. Bravo! Months or years have passed, and you're not receiving the traction you were expecting. As a matter of fact, you are feeling somewhat discouraged, and perhaps, you are ready to throw in the towel. Don't do it! Don't you quit! This is when you must dig deep and learn how to pivot. Let me explain.

First, let's define what I mean by pivoting your business. Companies do it all the time. In simple terms, pivoting is changing the direction of your products and services to generate more revenue. The end game is not just to survive in the market, but to thrive in the market! First, you must start with an inward reflection. Ask yourself questions like: How do I feel about the products and services I offer? Do I enjoy offering these services? What problems am I solving for my clients? Outside of the quantifiable data, you must evaluate your own interaction within your business.

But how do you know for sure it's time to pivot your business? Here are some big clues: Sales have stalled or dropped. You're not getting a response from your audience. Your perspective has changed. The passion is gone. Only one area of your business is getting traction. There's too much competition. No business can survive and thrive without customers.

All the changes I've made in my business were a direct result of listening to my customers and audience. If you haven't done an ideal customer analysis exercise in a while, do one asap! Interview some customers. Is there anything that they need or want that you're not providing but could? I assess my business every three months. This helps me to review all the processes of my business and evaluate what's working, what's not, and areas I can improve on. Know what your audience needs and wants and how you can help them achieve success! Remember to consider their pain points. Listen to your customers!

In entrepreneurship, you'll most likely pivot several times. This will save you time, effort, and money. Change doesn't have to be perfect, and it will never be smooth or comfortable. Just start making changes and improvise when necessary. Pick new goals to align with your new strategy and pivot as soon as you can. Now is the time to revisit your revenue and customer goals for your new strategy. Be realistic, but also give yourself a challenge. Outline exactly what needs to happen to meet your revenue goals.

Build upon the work you've already done. Your business will always be a work in progress. Just as markets grow and change, so will you. If I've had any regret in life, it's not starting my online business sooner.

Continue to Educate Yourself

The #1 skill needed by a successful entrepreneur is to be a continual learner. During my time working with online course creators, I've learned that the successful ones are continually learning either from past mistakes or just educating themselves on business and marketing skills.

There's so much information to learn (and learn quickly) when growing your online course business and I want to be here to help and support you.

While it's great to have content you can sit and read about creating and marketing an online course, you need an option to learn on the go. Subscribe to *The Course Creator's MBA* podcast on Apple Podcasts or your favorite podcast platform, where I cover actionable topics that you can implement immediately and see results in your business.

CPSIA information can be obtained
at www.ICGtesting.com
Printed in the USA
BVHW051411270423
663157BV00016B/691